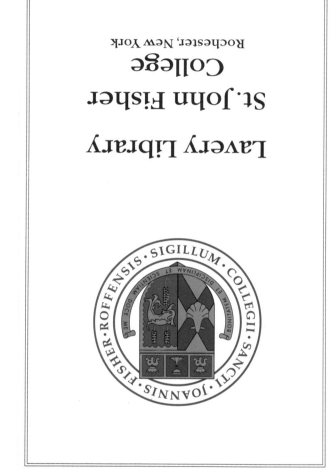

EDUCATION

FOR

THINKING

DEANNA KUHN

HARVARD UNIVERSITY PRESS

Cambridge, Massachusetts

London, England

2005

Library of Congress Cataloging-in-Publication Data

Kuhn, Deanna.
   Education for thinking / Deanna Kuhn.
      p. cm.
   Includes bibliographical references (p.) and index.
   ISBN 0-674-01906-7 (cloth : alk. paper)
   1. Thought and thinking—Study and teaching. 2. Inquiry-based learning. 3. Critical thinking in children. 4. Education—Aims and objectives. I. Title.

   LB1590.3.K84 2005
   372′.01′1—dc22   2005046321

For all of my children.
May you think well and often.

CONTENTS

INTRODUCTION

I

WHY GO TO SCHOOL? | 1

Why do we send our children to school? Answers to this question are both straightforward and elusive, objects of both widespread agreement and bitter dispute. We expect schools to prepare children for life. The years children spend in school are hard to justify as ends in themselves. Still, this traditional wisdom appears in need of reaffirmation today, having been voiced recently by such disparate figures as college presidents (Botstein, 1997) and cognitive psychologists (Anderson et al., 2000). Anderson and colleagues put it plainly, saying it is essential that we "develop a better understanding of relations between what is taught in classrooms and the capabilities children have and should develop in their present and future nonschool lives" (p. 12).

Broad visions of the kind of life preparation we would like education to accomplish are familiar and hard to quarrel with. We seek to produce students who will become "confident, eager, and self-motivated learners" and "responsible and independent thinkers," who will "love learning and value knowledge," who will be "open-minded and compassionate" and "fulfill their creative potential," who will gain "competence, self-reliance and self-knowledge," and who will display "self-assurance, curiosity, responsibility, independence and teamwork"—all of these are quotations from current brochures of premier public and independent schools. Or, put most simply and perhaps most convincingly in a report on the nation's middle schools, schools should help students "learn to use their minds well" (Jackson and Davis, 2000, p. 11). Who could disagree?

Any sense of widespread agreement rapidly evaporates, however, as soon as we get any more specific, seeking to translate the abstract ideals of mission statements into the particulars of what children should spend their time doing in school (and how that connects to what they will spend time doing as adults). It is indeed very hard to move from this level of abstraction to a level even slightly more specific. Why is this so?

One answer is that modern society is changing so fast that we cannot envision how our children will live in the future. We thus do not know how to prepare them for their adult lives and are able to identify educational objectives in only the broadest, most abstract of terms. Countering this view, however, are spokespeople from the business world, who unhesitatingly tell us the skills they need their employees to have, lamenting that they so often find them missing. Employers say they are looking for "smart" employees who can adapt to new circumstances, promptly assessing what they need to know and learning it, and who are able to engage in flexible teamwork to solve problems collaboratively (Murnane and Levy, 1996). In addressing the 2001 graduating class of Columbia Business School, the chairman of the board of Intuit told the graduates that the most important skill they had acquired in their MBA studies was the ability to work as members of a team. When the graduates themselves were surveyed regarding what the degree had provided them (Kuhn, unpublished), most mentioned this same skill.

Why haven't educators paid more attention to voices from the vocational world that identify skills that will matter on the job? If we know that working as a member of a team to solve a problem or achieve a goal is a skill that students will need in their future lives, in a broad array of workplaces, why wait until graduate school to introduce it?

There are likely multiple answers to these questions, some having to do with historically uneasy relations between the educational and business worlds, with business traditionally regarded as interested in students primarily as a resource in furthering its own goals and educators interested in students' intellectual development as a goal in its own right. But even when we turn to educators' lofty goals, as reflected in the mission statements quoted from earlier, matters do not become any clearer. A claim that lies at the heart of this book is that we lack sufficient understanding of what it means to be an "independent learner and thinker" (to quote the language of the brochures) to make this a readily implementable goal in classrooms today.

Making more concrete and specific, and hence more meaningful and realizable, the objective of helping students learn to use their minds well is a major purpose of this book. But first we need to be clear as to why this should be our objective in the first place. It is this question I address in this chapter. How does one justify developing the mind's capabilities, individually and in collaboration with others, as the central goal of education?

If education is appropriately regarded as preparation for life, the answer follows readily. From the perspective of the individual, the justification is that developing the mind is the best possible preparation for the often unpredictable demands and opportunities that life holds. From a societal perspective, the premise is that we should seek to develop individuals who can function effectively in and contribute maximally to society. To do so, we will claim, they need to be able, individually and collectively, to seek knowledge to solve problems and to achieve goals, to use reasoned argument to address issues and to make judgments, and to value these activities as the means to maximizing individual and social welfare. The core sets of intellectual skills that they must develop in order to fulfill these individual and social objectives, I propose, are the skills of inquiry (the topic of Part II) and of argument (the topic of Part III). The values associated with these skills are the topic of Chapter 2.

In the remainder of this chapter, I consider alternative answers to the question of what education should seek to achieve. The fact that school attendance is legally mandated signifies society's belief that schooling has a common purpose and provides a unifying experience for the great diversity of youth who come under its mandate. Increasing diversity makes identification of a universal purpose challenging at best. Nonetheless, we see today a reaffirmation of the ideal of a unifying experience in the No Child Left Behind Act, affirming every child's right to become educated. If society is prepared to invest extraordinary effort and resources to ensure that no child is left behind, the assumption is that we have a very clear idea where all these children are headed and are confident that the destination is a worthy one and warrants the investment in the journey. It is a fitting time, then, to reexamine the purposes of education, in a framework of alternatives, and be certain of them. There are at least four different proposals, it turns out, significantly different from the one proposed here, as to what universal education should aspire to do. Each of these, I will conclude, is less defensible than the one I have proposed.

Educating to Instill Knowledge

Can knowledge be a bad thing? Are not children better off the more they know of the technical and social complexity of the modern world? This very complexity makes it essential, however, to take on the difficult question of which specific knowledge they need most. It is clearer today than it ever has been that we can hope to acquaint children with at most a tiny fraction of what there is to know, and we are hard pressed to predict which knowledge will be most useful to them.

How, then, to choose? Proposals vary on two dimensions, specificity and depth. At one extreme on the specificity dimension are the ideas of Hirsch

(1987), who has undertaken to identify in detail the exact bodies of knowledge an educated person should possess. At the other end of this dimension are educators such as Gardner (1999), who identify broad disciplinary domains that students should become acquainted with. Some, like Gardner, are concerned about students' depth of understanding within knowledge domains, while others, like Hirsch, do not see this as an issue.

Efforts like Hirsch's to itemize the specific knowledge that defines an educated person have become increasingly hard to defend. The overrepresentation of dead white males (DWMs) in classical lists of great works has now received enough attention that it has become clear that every group can (and is likely to) advance its own list (Graff, 1992). Moreover, lists like Hirsch's are a moving target. Almost 10 percent of the 6,900 entries in *The New Dictionary of Cultural Literacy* (Hirsch, Kett, and Trefil, 2002) are new, having not appeared in the earlier edition of the previous decade. How, then, can we advocate today's list as essential preparation for tomorrow's world? And perhaps most compelling, we need do no more than think about what proportion of the knowledge imparted in our own junior high school classes we can remember, and it becomes difficult to make the case for any *particular* body of factual knowledge as essential to becoming educated.

But this is not to say that factual knowledge itself is unimportant. It is just that the emphasis needs to shift. If, as Gardner's (1999) views imply, one Dickens novel versus another or one Mozart opera versus another may suit a teacher's instructional purposes equally well and can be expected to yield comparable educational benefits, then both novels (or operas) must be serving some further purpose, distinguishable from what is derived from study of either one itself. We thus move into the domain of skill development and the knotty issue of transfer. We involve students with some body of knowledge not as an end in itself (because we could as well have employed another), but because we hope they will acquire something further from the experience. The involvement will provide a needed foundation, open doors, make other achievements possible.

Educating to Develop Skills

The concept of education as skill development comes much closer to the conception advocated in this book. But the concept is a broad one, and we immediately confront the same questions we encountered in contemplating education as knowledge acquisition. What kinds of skills and to what end? Why these skills and not others? Skills can be as specific as use of a dictionary or ruler or as broad as the "habits of mind" identified by Meier

(1995) or "thinking dispositions" described by Perkins and colleagues (Perkins, Jay, and Tishman, 1993), although both of the latter merge into values, the topic we turn to in the next chapter. Still, one must have the skills needed to exercise the habits of mind or modes of thinking that one may value and hence be disposed to practice. If we are to get beyond generalities, we need to know fairly specifically what these skills are. How are they to be defined in terms specific enough to be useful and yet general enough to be more than descriptions of particular activities alleged to require them?

In his book *Education in the Knowledge Age,* Bereiter (2002) takes a spirited and tough stand on the topic of intellectual skills. He decries the "word magic" that he sees as rampant, reflected in the assumption that anything that is learned will automatically transfer to everything else known by the same name. Educators, for example, take for granted that engaging young children in an activity that involves classifying objects will teach something known as classification skill and, in so doing, enhance mastery of any other activity that shares this label.

To maintain categorically, as does Bereiter, that there exists no evidence for transfer (of experience from one activity to another) is perhaps an overly simplistic response to a set of complex conceptual and empirical questions. A violinist is likely to progress more rapidly than a flutist in learning the cello. A student taking her fifth course in English literature is likely to exhibit more skill in analyzing character and plot than the one taking her first. Yet, Bereiter is right that educators cannot take transfer as a matter of faith. To accept Bereiter's hard line on the transfer question is to impose the formidable burden of face validity on the educator. In the face of complex and sometimes conflicting data on transfer from researchers, this is for now probably the right position for educators to assume. It means that any educational activity in which they involve students must have face validity in its own right. In other words, its value must be clear and apparent from the activity itself. It cannot be maintained that the value of the activity lies in its potential to enhance performance of some other kind of activity. Despite optimistic claims to the contrary, neither Latin nor algebra nor any other subject has been demonstrated to "improve the mind."

The concept of education as skill development, then, must for the time being remain promissory. Students certainly do develop and make use of intellectual skills. Yet much of the analytic work—both conceptual and empirical—remains to be done. What precisely are the intellectual skills that students ought to acquire, and in what kinds of activities can they be identified? And—a question I have already broached—what justification do we have for singling out certain skills over others as worthy of educational investment? Assuming these questions can be answered satisfactorily, we confront the further task of determining how best to ensure students' mastery of these skills. And even if we meet with success in this respect, there remains yet a further challenge. Will students see these skills as worth exercising once instructional support is withdrawn and they resume autonomous control of their own behavior? Will they understand when, where, and why to use them? These questions invoke the topic of intellectual values, which we take up in Chapter 2. In Parts II and III of the book, we examine in detail the skills themselves that are proposed as worthy educational goals.

Educating for Selection

Should education seek to increase the commonality among people, by providing a universal set of experiences, or should it increase the differences among them, by selecting those most suited to more advanced, specialized kinds of education while judging others as less qualified for these pursuits? Although the institution of legally mandated, universal education suggests the first purpose, education can and is likely to continue to serve the dual functions of "leveler" and "sorter." The question is more one of *how* it serves these functions. However fine a system of universal education might be devised, everyone cannot learn everything and decisions must somehow be made as to how individuals and specialized forms of education will be matched.

Much, however, has been found to criticize of late regarding operation of the selection function. The most serious charge is that selection has assumed a role of unacceptable proportion, becoming the tail wagging the educational dog. At the extreme, it supplants entirely the education for which students are being selected. According to some, for example, employers value the MBA degree more as a selection device of individuals suited to succeed in the corporate world than as a vehicle for students to learn anything they will need there. If so, why not simply administer the selection process and forget the costly two-year program to which applicants have been admitted (or not)?

One factor in judging the advisability of this move is whether the tests that accomplish the selection are any good. Here, there is no reason for great confidence. From the advanced tests that determine entry into graduate degree programs, to the now famed Scholastic Assessment Test (SAT) on which high school students' fates depend, to the standardized tests that are rapidly assuming a key place in public elementary education, and even to the tests that play a role in admission to selective schools by children as young as four, criticism is sharp and abundant, with few beyond the test-makers taking on the role of apologists for the tests.

The idea behind most of these tests is that they measure what psychologists have traditionally called an "aptitude," which in turn is expected to predict the likely degree of achievement in the arena in which the aptitude is being assessed. Modern psychologists concerned with individual differences, such as Sternberg (1998), however, eschew the distinction between assessing aptitude and assessing achievement. If we want to know whether someone will make a good lawyer or CEO, Sternberg maintains, we are better off with even a brief sampling of their behavior in which they are asked to do lawyer-like or CEO-like things, rather than relying on paper-and-pencil tests that have been shown to be at best weak predictors of the behaviors of interest.

If the tests are not serving this predictive function, or not serving it well, we should not feel at ease according them the societal role they play as selection devices. And the more power they wield, the more uneasy we should become. We may worry less about the justice of who gains the privilege of boasting the high-status MBA credential and whether those not selected might have performed just as well on the job. But there is growing evidence that at the less rarefied level of public elementary education, standardized tests of increasing number and frequency of administration are influencing the fate not just of individual children but of classrooms, teachers, principals, and district superintendents. To the extent this is happening, we should be concerned about whether the tests are assessing what we believe and can justify is important to assess.

One rarely hears impassioned defenses of existing standardized tests as measures of educational achievement. Are there better assessments that we would like to replace them? We can only begin to answer this question if we have a clear sense of what the goal is, what we expect education to achieve. If public education is to overcome its preoccupation with standardized test scores, we need an improved vision of what it means to be an educated person. In the final chapter, we ask to what extent the ideas in this book contribute to that goal.

Despite the acknowledged dual functions of education, objectives must take precedence over selection. It is hard to envision and justify the selection function (to more variable individual educational pathways) in the absence of a firm sense of universal objectives. The function of selection cannot stand alone. We can employ anything from a ten-minute multiple-choice test to a four-year-or-longer degree program to select the "best and brightest" to fill society's most prestigious roles. But the tests themselves cannot tell us what we want these individuals, arguably society's most precious resource, to know or be able to do, except in the most circular of ways. Indeed, without clear objectives that stand on their own, distinct from the test, the risk of circularity looms large.

Two examples stand out, at opposite ends of the educational spectrum. One involves admission to the highly selective military academies (West Point, the Naval Academy, and the Air Force Academy). Applicants who are promising but do not make the point cut-off for admission may be offered financial aid to attend an external preparatory academy. Its four-month program focuses almost entirely on raising students' SAT scores to the levels required for academy admission. Attendees, for example, memorize twenty vocabulary words a day and take SAT tests once a month. Clearly, this is a case in which performance on a test meant to serve as a predictor of performance has become an end in itself. The officials involved appear to have succumbed to a kind of "score magic" akin to the "word magic" that Bereiter (2002) disparages. Applicants who raise their scores on the selection test to the required level have somehow become better suited to face the rigors of academy life.

A second example comes from the public elementary school level. Although only a few school districts were involved, the mentality the example reflects is typical. In the summer of 2002, several Florida school districts announced that they would begin the school year a week earlier than usual so teachers would have time to cover what students needed to know for the standardized tests in December. This stance reflects more than teaching to the test, or the testing tail wagging the educational dog. The tests defined the school's mission, its raison d'être. Surely we need a better source of wisdom as to where we as a society wish to head, for it is toward that end that we should be preparing our youth.

Ironically, the current preoccupation with standardized test scores, motivated by concern over the quality of the educational system, is probably the single greatest factor that will constrain its development over the next decade. To make the conceptual progress that stands the best chance of improving education, we need to put aside standardized test scores, and the many studies of the variables that affect them, and look to life outside of and beyond school as a source of wisdom regarding what our children should learn.

Educating for Citizenship

Universal public education is charged with providing a unifying experience for the enormous diversity of children who come under its jurisdiction.

Defining that unifying experience is far from straightforward. By the age of five or six, children have already had extraordinarily diverse sets of experiences that they bring to their first encounters with compulsory schooling. And they are destined for an even greater diversity of adult lives. What common, "unifying" educational experience during the years of mandatory schooling can best prepare them for the futures they face?

Education for citizenship has been one traditional answer to this demanding question. Citizenship is a role shared by all members of a democratic society, and it is in the interest of any such society that its members engage this role in a responsible and effective manner. But what is required, in today's complex and troubled world, to ensure this outcome? Other nations, we've been told, are educating their youth to regard American society as the path of evil and to act on these beliefs. In such a climate, are democratic societies not justified, perhaps even obligated, to educate their children to thoroughly know and respect the set of values and traditions on which their own society is founded? Is this not a sufficiently clear and noble mission for education in any society?

This path, it turns out, is not all that clear and, moreover, is fraught with complications and its own set of dangers. Prominent among them is the temptation to embark on the slippery slope of sanitizing the stories we tell students, so as to tell these stories "our way." Decisions range from minor ones of omission or emphasis to major ones of which story is told. Do we want students to study the founding of the United States from the perspective of the Native Americans, the British, or only the colonial settlers?

And what about all of the ideas and values that do not fit with our own? Fierce debates now abound revolving around whether we want our youth to be exposed to, or protected from, alien ideas. Students should learn about the concept of evolution, most (though not all) American citizens agree, but do they need to learn about Islam and its beliefs? In the end, to include the "core beliefs and values" of a society as a foundation of its compulsory public school curriculum, we would have to achieve a near-perfect degree of clarity and consensus not only as to what these beliefs and values are, but also as to how best to transmit them to a new generation. Interpreted in this way, education for citizenship is a tall order.

A more flexible, and forgiving, version of education for citizenship is to prepare youths to engage in effective debate of the issues that arise in a democratic society that coexists with a diversity of other societies in a complex world. In the case of American society, this is a commitment that is broader, certainly, than a commitment to "the American way," yet one entirely compatible with core American values.

To the extent such an objective is achieved, the need and rationale for more specific and restrictive forms of civic education recede. Students well educated to engage in effective debate are able to construct, or reconstruct, for themselves the rationales on which democratic societies are founded, without the requirement of absolute uniformity in the conceptual edifices that are constructed.

But to adopt this solution is to bring us back to the topic that is the central one of this book—education for thinking. To prepare our youth to engage in effective debate of the important issues that arise in their local and global communities is to prepare them to think well, individually and especially collaboratively, and to value doing so, as a means of maximizing individual and societal welfare. In the remainder of the book, we examine what it means to think well, how good thinking develops, and how educators can support this development. Education for citizenship, we can conclude, depends not on the inculcation of any particular set of ideas or values but rather on development of the cognitive capabilities that enable citizens to participate in the ongoing debate that democratic societies require. We turn finally, then, to education for thinking.

Educating for Thinking

Educating for thinking, the educational mission advocated in this book, is no small or straightforward task. To even begin to realize it, we must achieve greater clarity than exists now as to the path that leads to good thinking, to minds being well used. Indeed, we must first understand exactly what good thinking is, in the real-life contexts in which it matters. In reaction to the latter objective, some educators may say, "We all know good thinking when we see it; let's not get bogged down trying to agree on definitions and let's concentrate instead on the more interesting, important challenge of devising the educational environments that will make it likely to appear." Given the prevalence of this stance, educators today are more likely to agree on promising educational activities and settings for fostering thinking than on what the thinking skills are that they seek to induce in these settings. They may end up having much to say about *how*, but relatively little about *what*, it is important for students to achieve.

I take strong exception to this stance, arguing instead that we need to know fairly precisely what a cognitive skill is if we hope to teach it or create the conditions for its development. Accordingly, I have devoted much of my research in the field of cognitive development to better understanding two major families of thinking skills that I contend constitute a core of effective thinking and that are the topics of Parts II and III of this book—the skills of inquiry and the skills of argument. In these two parts of the book, I undertake to identify in precise (although not overly technical) psychological terms what at least elementary mastery of these skills entails.

Many readers will be aware of the large, long-standing literature on the topic of critical thinking and may therefore ask, "Don't we already know by now what critical thinking is?" What this book brings to the debate is based on three characteristics that set it apart from previous writing on thinking and education. First, as a research psychologist, I have firmly based the book's claims on empirical evidence (in contrast to the bulk of the literature on critical thinking, which largely lacks such a foundation). Second, this evidence is developmental in nature, tracing how the cognitive skills in question evolve from their initial emergent to their most highly evolved forms. Identifying the processes and paths by means of which skilled thinking emerges is the first step, I claim, before we can go on to devise the best ways to support that development. Existing literature on thinking skills for the most part does not adopt a developmental perspective.

Third, the book situates thinking in contexts of students' current and prospective concerns and purposes beyond the classroom, with a focus on education for life. Because so much research on thinking is devoted to thinking about artificial content constructed for research purposes or to students' thinking about the academic content of the school curriculum, we know comparatively little about the thinking skills that are exercised in everyday, nonacademic settings and, especially, the manner in which these skills develop. Yet I have argued in this chapter that developing these skills—the skills that will equip students for life's demands and opportunities—should be the focus of educators' efforts. If this is their objective, to undertake it educators need more of a knowledge base regarding how such skills develop than provided by the educational psychology courses that have been a staple of teacher education programs. It is at least the foundations of such a knowledge base that I seek to provide in this book.

Thinking as a Social Activity

Thinking skills are typically regarded as intellectual competencies that educators endeavor to instill in students' heads so these competencies are available for use when needed. The concept of thinking skills adopted here contrasts sharply with this traditional one. Thinking is something people *do,* most often collaboratively, while they are engaged in pursuing the activities and goals that fill their daily lives. Thinking rarely remains a solitary activity conducted inside people's heads. Thinking is most often and most importantly a social activity, embodied in the discourse people engage in to advance their individual and shared goals.

We also need to ask why the particular thinking skills highlighted in this book, inquiry and argument, deserve the attention I claim they do. At this juncture, I can do no more than try to anticipate a full answer, which awaits further investigation of the skills themselves. The fuller answer unfolds in the remainder of the book. It incorporates aspects of both the skills and the citizenship perspectives examined in this chapter. To produce individuals who can thrive in and contribute maximally to a democratic society, we need to ensure they develop the intellectual skills needed to inquire and to argue, individually and collectively, and to value these activities as the soundest path to achieving goals, solving problems, resolving conflicts, and maximizing individual and group welfare.

Fully important as the cognitive skills themselves are the values that support them, because these values govern the extent to which the skills will be applied and practiced. If we regard thinking as something people do in the context of purposeful activity (rather than as a hidden competency they possess), we can see that people are likely to employ more demanding thinking skills only to the extent that they appreciate their value. Consciously or unconsciously, they will choose the most effective and efficient ways to achieve their purposes. If the education for thinking advocated in this book is to be effective, those who experience it must embrace a set of beliefs and values that hold the skills of inquiry and argument to be worth the effort they entail because they are the most promising means of solving problems, enhancing well-being, and furthering goals. In Chapter 2, we take a closer look at these beliefs and values, in an effort to understand what they are and how they develop, before proceeding in Parts II and III to the intellectual skills needed to implement these values.

Because this book's treatment of its topic is empirical, this introductory chapter needs to identify the kind of empirical evidence that is drawn on. Some is published research data by the author and by other cognitive, developmental, and educational psychologists. But most academic research removes thinking and learning from its natural contexts. If thinking is social and collaborative, as I have stressed, examining the actual social settings in which it occurs is critical. Sections of each of the next chapters are therefore devoted to observations conducted by the author in two middle-school Social Studies classrooms at very different schools over the course of the same semester. In each class, the teacher's expressed objectives were strikingly consistent with those identified in this chapter—developing skills of collaboration, inquiry, and argument—allowing us a view of what goes on in classrooms today in the name of those activities. This is essential information to have, for any proposals we may make ought to take current practice as a starting point.

The two classrooms I chose were from opposite ends of the educational spectrum and could not have been more different. Described in more detail in Chapter 2, one classroom is in an inner-city public school we euphemistically labeled the "struggling school" and the other in a suburban public school we labeled the "best-practice school." The latter label is intended not to reflect my own assessment of the school's practices but rather the way in which the school is viewed by the larger community. The school is widely regarded as providing the best education, public or private, that educators know how to deliver. In fact, I found both classrooms far from the educational ideal that I propose in this book's concluding chapter, though in very different ways. In the environment of New York City and its suburbs, where these observations were conducted, the majority of schools fall closer to one or the other of these ends of the educational spectrum, with fewer instances occupying the middle ground between them. Although this picture is different in other parts of the United States, I chose to focus on the two ends of the continuum in the belief that they would be the most illuminating. The goal of No Child Left Behind (NCLB) is that every child successfully navigate the path of universal schooling and profit from all it has to offer, and students at the heartbreakingly large number of urban schools like the struggling school are the ones NCLB is intended to rescue. The best-practice classroom, in turn, is supposed to reveal exactly that—it is a model of current educational practice at its best, perhaps even what NCLB might aspire to for every child.

The education for thinking proposed in this book, then, has several minimal criteria it must fulfill. It must be feasible and justifiable as a curriculum for students at both ends of the educational spectrum, thus providing the unifying objective necessary to justify universal compulsory education. Its virtues, relative to the status quo of prevailing practice for either group, must be clear. And, to conclude this chapter where it began, its value must derive from its effectiveness as education for life. To this tall order, we now turn our attention.

Effective education, as noted in Chapter 1, encompasses not just skills but values. Education, in the end, is about changing beliefs, and beliefs, Olson (2003) reminds us, are intentional states. Only the holder of a belief can decide to change that belief. Ultimately, then, it is the student who must make sense of the educational mission—and must buy into it—if it is to have any chance of success at all. We cannot introduce ourselves as a presence in students' lives, determined to educate them whether they like it or not. They will decide what is worth learning and knowing. They will make whatever meaning is to be made from what schools and teachers present to them. And they are the ones to decide what is relevant to their purposes and therefore will be taken away from the experience and what will be cast aside.

In short, values derive from the thinking and feeling of the valuer. They are not imposed from without. It is the student's experience, then, that must be at the forefront of our analysis, and so we begin with that experience here.

Making Meaning of School

We can require that students attend school, but we cannot dictate what sense they make of what goes on there. The one thing we can be sure of is that students make *some* sense of the school life that absorbs so much of their time. They figure out what is going on. The danger is that the meaning students construct may end up being quite different from what educators would like it to be.

Is there reason to think this is so? We have little systematic evidence to go on. For all of their conscientious efforts to teach their students, teachers (at any level, from kindergarten through college) do not often consider what their students *think* they are learning and why they think it might, or might not, make sense to learn it. Yet students' ideas about these matters are likely to play a critical role in what they take away from the many hours they spend in classrooms. If students cannot answer the question, "Why would I want or need to know this?" they will find it difficult to direct more than superficial attention to what is being taught. Even if they remember the information for a test, it remains unconnected to anything else they think about or know and inevitably will soon be forgotten.

Even more significant than what is forgotten, however, is what a student does come to understand, and is likely to long remember, about what takes place in a schoolroom. Based to a large extent on their own school experiences, children form conceptions of what learning is about that may well last a lifetime. The prevailing emphasis on standardized test preparation and performance, particularly in low-performing schools, makes one likely conception of learning that of drilling arbitrary information into memory to pass tests. To the extent this conception is dominant, it is not hard to envision academically at-risk students—the ones most in need of discovering what learning and education are about—concluding "this isn't for me." Once formed, such beliefs are likely to remain intact over a lifetime, perhaps even passed on to another generation.

It seems essential, then, that we begin with students' own ideas about schooling and learning, especially if we think these may be worthy of change. Potential influences on such concepts extend, of course, beyond students' personal classroom experience to families, communities, and media. Moreover, we cannot talk about the influence of classroom experience without focusing investigation on particular kinds of schools in particular communities, because the realities, in sharp contrast to the ideals, of the American educational system reveal enormous and disconcerting differences in the school experiences of students from different sectors of society.

In this chapter, and continuing in later chapters, I draw on interviews and classroom observations I conducted in two public middle schools that lie at opposite ends on a continuum of perceived quality, one serving what we have come to call a "disadvantaged" population and the other serving a highly advantaged one. Neither school is by any means a statistical rarity, especially at the low end of the continuum, although in examining schools near the ends, I admittedly do not depict many schools that lie nearer the middle of this continuum. My observations focus on two Social Studies classes, a seventh-grade class in what I refer to as the "best-practice" school and an eighth-grade class in what I refer to as the "struggling" school.

The "struggling" school is an inner-city public middle school in New York City that serves a largely African-American and Hispanic population, all of whom are regarded as "academically at risk." Sadly, it is characteristic of the majority of inner-city public schools in large urban areas. Based on the number of students qualifying for subsidized school meals, the economic level of families is low. Academic achievement is also low, with only a small percentage of students performing at grade level in mathematics or language arts and few likely to achieve any degree of academic success, based on the records of previous graduates. Most have already become disengaged and disinterested in schoolwork. Academic work in language arts and mathematics focuses on the basic skills required to pass mandated standardized tests. The physical environment of the school is spare but acceptable, except for overcrowding. The school is well equipped with computer hardware and software obtained through various grant programs. All students have access to computers, printers, and the Internet. In the eighth-grade Social Studies class I observed, the teacher was a soft-spoken, pleasant, conscientious young woman in her third year of teaching.

The "best-practice" school is a premier public school of national reputation in an affluent New York City suburb. The community is one in which parents and children enjoy substantial economic advantage, and parents are highly educated (in the majority of families, at least one parent has a postgraduate degree) and heavily invested in their children's education. Expectation and achievement levels are exceptionally high, with average SAT scores of graduating seniors among the county's highest. All of the school's graduates go to college, most to Ivy League schools or other prestigious liberal arts colleges. In the seventh-grade Social Studies class I observed, the teacher was an energetic, dedicated middle-aged woman who had taught seventh-grade Social Studies at the school for more than a decade.

In each school, I observed on average once per week, over the course of a semester, one particular class of the several equivalent Social Studies classes taught by the teacher. I also spent lesser amounts of time observing in other classrooms and schools similar to these two, enough so as to be confident that each was not dissimilar from a larger number of its type. In this chapter, I draw on these observations, as well as on interviews with students themselves and their parents and teachers, to explore the meanings that students of the two schools attribute to their school experience. In later chapters, I draw further on observations in these two classrooms; and in the concluding chapter, I consider their implications in relation to the objectives of education for thinking and education for life, which form this book's theme.

Observations of School Life at the Struggling School

My dominating impression of the struggling school was its noise level. The corridors, especially between classes, were hazardous as well as noisy. At any given time, in any corridor, I would see two or three physical encounters between students that were sometimes controlled and playful, but sometimes not. We observed one major fistfight in the school cafeteria that required uniformed guard intervention. The fight was particularly memorable because the students involved were at the time under the supervision of my research assistants and me, as we conducted the work described in Part III. Adults, particularly outsiders, in the corridors between classes tended to walk with their hands out slightly to the front of them to protect themselves from being jostled by students' shoving one another.

The high activity level and frequency of physical encounters are perhaps not surprising given the amount of time students spend in the corridors. As a routine practice, students were required to line up in the corridor outside of the classroom they were leaving, wait until a supervising teacher signaled that they were in order, and then proceed in single file, as a group, to the next class. (Each class of students moved as a group through a uniform sequence of classes.) On arrival they had to again assemble in line outside the classroom until a teacher signaled that they were all in conformity with behavior standards and could enter the classroom.

Given the short (forty-three-minute) class periods and hence frequent class changes, a good proportion of school time (perhaps 20 percent overall) was spent in the corridor between classes. Complying with the prescribed norm of standing in line silently during these periods of time, avoiding any interactions with others, required more self-control than all but a very few students showed. At least one and usually more than one student in each of these corridor line-ups required disciplinary correction. An adult, shouting to be heard, would turn attention to correcting an individual student, during which time one or more other students would misbehave and attract the adult's attention. Typically, after two or three of these individual corrections, students were directed to file into class.

Within the classroom I observed, the noise level was reduced but still substantial. Of the thirty-five students in the class, twenty-eight to thirty were present on any given day. It was unusual for the class to be silent or to hear only a single person speaking. At any given time, a number of students were likely to be talking, sometimes loudly, or laughing. Teachers and other adults at the school were accustomed to attracting students' attention with some form of loud noise or speaking in a raised voice—shouting, in fact—to make themselves heard. In the classroom, after the teacher gained the students' attention, she had to struggle to maintain it, which she was rarely able to do for more than a couple of minutes. Maintaining enough order to allow her agenda to proceed was a major, perhaps the major, challenge. Typically, the teacher was willing to continue with what she was saying if no more than two or three individual conversations were going on softly and the majority of students were quiet. After a few minutes of presiding over the class, she gave in-class assignments to be completed individually, in pairs, or occasionally in small groups, usually for the remainder of the period. During this time, her role became one of circulating among the students as they worked, although on several occasions I observed her to leave the room for periods of ten to fifteen minutes.

It quickly became apparent that the agendas of students at the struggling school were largely at odds with those of teachers. First on their agenda was to stay below the radar of any of the adults in the environment so they could pursue the rest of their agenda, which had nothing to do with the teacher's objectives and was largely social in nature. As an adult immediately perceived to be in the opposing camp, I was able to catch only glimpses of the rich and lively social agenda that took place throughout the school day. Adults were an obstacle to be circumvented in advancing this agenda. Students and staff quite clearly did not have a common purpose. They were not on the same team.

The struggling-school students I observed were adept at staying below the teacher's radar. They had learned ways to appear to be paying at least intermittent attention to their work, while at the same time pursuing an entirely different agenda. In later chapters, I examine the teacher's agenda—the kinds of activities that she selected for her class. Often, what students at the struggling school were being asked to do was beyond them and they had little alternative but to appear to engage the task. Even when an activity was within their grasp, however, students were likely to give it little more attention than needed to avoid being singled out for disciplinary attention. Despite the teacher's frequent exhortations to finish an in-class assignment, there was little sense of task completion as providing any desired closure. Instead, closure was provided by the bell students knew would ring when forty-three minutes had elapsed. They packed up and anticipated that bell at least several minutes before it rang, and I had the clear impression that they would not give another thought to the goings-on of that classroom until they reentered it the next day.

The fundamental problem seemed to me to be that students at the struggling school had not bought in to the school enterprise. They were present because they had been told they had to be, and they were resigned, for the time being, to this constraint on their activities and lives. By all appearances, the students did not worry themselves with trying to find out why adults were making this demand, even though the demand did not make a lot of sense to them. They either never had or had lost their trust in teachers as adults who had their interests at heart and could be counted on not to waste their time with pointless activities. Within this setting, students endeavored to make the best of their situation and to follow their own agendas within its constraints.

For all the other disadvantages and challenges, then, that plagued the struggling school and so many others like it, there was another: Teachers did not serve as the leaders, guides, or role models that we would have wished them to be along a path of learning. For them to have assumed any such role, the teachers would have had to be perceived by students as on the same team—as sharing the same goals that the students had—rather than as adversaries whose purposes conflicted with their own.

Observations of School Life at the Best-Practice School

At the best-practice school, the atmosphere could not have been more different. The fact that the number of students (eighteen to twenty) in a classroom was about half that in a classroom of the same size in the struggling school is of course an important factor in accounting for the difference. But students at the best-practice school seemed not to even think of disrupting the classroom agenda with off-task behavior. Discipline was simply not an issue in daily classroom life. Like students at the struggling school, students were concerned about how they looked and clearly took care in their dress to project certain images, but these matters of dress and appearance did not receive attention that distracted from the classroom agenda. Neither did the social concerns these students had intrude into the classroom. Behavior infractions did occur at the school and were addressed, but at another time and place than the classroom.

The dominating characteristic was not noise, as in the struggling school, but time, which was treated as a precious commodity not to be wasted. Students rushed from one class to the next in the few minutes allotted. Help sessions, after-school sports, and other activities kept most at school until five o'clock or later, at which point they headed for home with weighty packs of books that would demand several hours of evening attention. The daily schedule reflected a carefully negotiated agreement among staff in the various subject-matter areas regarding how many minutes (in a six-day cycle, because there was too much to cover in a five-day week) their subject warranted. None of the precious minutes would ever be wasted lining up in corridors.

Why, in marked contrast to the atmosphere in the struggling-school classroom, was it understood and accepted that nonacademic concerns were relegated to times and places outside the classroom? Part of the answer seems to be that the classroom agenda was sufficiently full and demanding to absorb students' full attention almost all of the time. Activities were sometimes teacher centered and sometimes student centered; but in either case, students were observed to be attentive and to apply themselves with considerable industry. The sense that pervaded the classroom was that there was work that needed to be done.

This sense was reinforced by abundant indicators that students would be accountable for accomplishing that work. Daily homework assignments, usually reading and preparation of review sheets, were a given. These were collected and reviewed by the teacher and returned for inclusion in the carefully organized notebooks that students relied on in preparing for major tests every several weeks, as well as smaller quizzes that took place at least weekly. The focus on assessment of performance was intense. Each piece of work was reviewed, and usually commented on, by the teacher. Students were aware how the various forms of assessment contributed to their final grade and of their own standing in the class and what they had to do to maintain or improve it.

What motivated these preteens to commit themselves so impressively to this undertaking? The topic during the weeks I observed, life in the early American colonies, was not a terribly exciting one; and these privileged youth had many activities that competed for their time outside of school. Yet, uncompleted homework was infrequent. Home environments clearly played a role. Parents had come to accept nightly homework as a given, beginning in the early grades; and in the vast majority of these students' homes, the expectation that children would undertake and complete all assigned work was an extension of the expectations that governed life at school. And many parents felt the need to do more than provide an appropriate environment and expectations. Private tutors for these seventh graders were common in all subjects, including Social Studies, which was widely regarded as the most difficult seventh-grade subject. In addition, the school held daily extra help sessions and, for many students, provided skill center and resource room support. In sharp contrast to the shame associated with the "learning disabled" label in many schools, at this best-practice school (and most others like it), having one's child identified as having "learning differences" and hence in need of extra resources was widely considered by parents as a victory to be regarded with pride, an extra arrow in a child's scholastic quiver.

As they engaged industriously in their best-practice classrooms, and later at their desks at home at night, what sense did these young students have of "why would I want or need to know this?" The answer is a clear one, certainly no secret to the students, parents, or teachers and principals involved in the effort, and that answer is "to get into a top college." By the sophomore year, getting into college was the most common topic of conversation among the school's students and parents alike, and the school introduced the college application process, and all of the preparation leading up to it, in that year. Decisions to engage or not engage in an activity were commonly made based on "how it will look for college," and evidence of these concerns extended down to the middle school, where students' enrollment in accelerated sequences in math, science, and foreign language would affect how many advanced placement courses they would be able to take in high school.

Thus, high performance expectations were made explicit both at home and at school, and the large majority of students accepted the word of the adults around them that the effort was worth it. In sharp contrast to the skeptical adolescents at the struggling school, who regarded adults largely as obstacles to their agendas, students at the best-practice school accepted that their parents and teachers had their best interests at heart and were guiding them along the path to success. Students, parents, and teachers were all on the same team, working toward the same goals, despite intense competition among students to reach and stay near the front of the pack.

Making School Make Sense

Would the advantaged students in the best-practice school ever contemplate why educational achievements open the doors to status and privilege? Or had they taken it for granted for so long that the question never occurred to them? If it did, would they assume the doors opened to the best students as winners of a contest that proved them more able than others (the "sorter," in contrast to "leveler," function of education)? Would they see education as a competition in which the most able take the best prizes?

Or, possibly, would these students, and their parents, see their current and future educational experiences as providing them with something worth having, beyond the diploma or the degree itself? Neither the students nor parents I talked to seemed to have a clear idea of what that "something" might be. Parents want to make sure their children attend the best middle and high schools less because of what they'll learn there than because they are such a widely recognized path to the best colleges. Students are too busy and pressured to think much about it.

As a result, any quest to find personal meaning or value in educational pursuits was largely set aside at the best-practice school. The purpose of school was to qualify for more schooling. The vaguely defined sense of promised pay-off lay down the road. In marked contrast to their disadvantaged counterparts, who could not buy into school, the privileged students at the best-practice school could not see their way beyond school.

This state of affairs has the implicit acceptance of the educators who direct and staff high-performing middle and high schools. The goal of the academically oriented high school is to excel in preparing students for the curriculum they will face in college. For the advantaged students at these schools, then, the challenge of finding any genuine meaning in educational pursuits is postponed to the extended adolescence that the college and even postcollege years have become. But it is not resolved, anymore than it is for the less-advantaged population who struggle to make any sense at all of their school experience and are likely to end it at an early age.

Although the two schools portrayed here are by no means isolated extremes, as I acknowledged earlier there is a large middle ground of American public schooling that fits neither of these portrayals and lies somewhere between them. Yet over the past several decades, public schools have become more and more polarized into haves and have-nots. There is pressure in suburban communities to make their schools more like the best-practice school, as indexed by quantifiable indicators like SAT scores and, directly correlated with those indicators, real estate values. At the same time, the problems of inner-city schools become more and more intractable.

Box 2.1 lists a sampling of the responses to the question we posed individually to twenty randomly selected students from both the struggling and the best-practice schools: "Are the things you are learning in school going to be of any value to you once you have finished your schooling?" The results are striking and paradoxical. The hard-working students from the best-practice school were the ones who expressed cynicism about the value of their studies, not the struggling-school students who exhibited so little day-to-day interest in their schoolwork. The best-practice students knew that school is the prescribed path to their future—college and careers—and they showed some sophistication, even, in abstracting broad personal traits and skills of those most likely to be successful. At the same time, they were often cynical about the value of the specifics that filled their daily academic schedules. Despite their certainty that school is the path to life success, they were not sure how or why school learning connects to life beyond school.

Students at the struggling school, in contrast, who devoted minimal attention or effort to schoolwork during school hours, and presumably even less outside of school, expressed no cynicism—at least overtly to an adult outsider—regarding the value of school. Their responses to our question displayed none of the cynicism and alienation apparent in their everyday school behavior. They went through the motions of what the school environment demanded of them, without a clear sense of how these demands related to their future lives. Yet they accepted, or at least were prepared to parrot back, what they have been told by adults in their lives: Education gets you ahead.

Reviewing the two sets of responses in Box 2.1 reveals little overlap between them. Only one struggling school student even mentioned college and then only in connection with getting admitted. For best-practice students, "getting in" was a given; they were concerned with doing well once accepted. A deep irony lies in the contrast between these two sets of responses. The belief that the struggling-school students expressed in the value of education will, for the majority, never be fulfilled. The education they are receiving is not in fact a secure path to a solid future. Very few, if any, will become the businessmen, accountants, or translators they expressed vague ideas about. Best-practice students, in contrast, voiced much more cynicism about the education that will, in almost all cases, lead them to bright and secure futures.

Buying into Intellectual Life

Should we worry about the connection that students draw between school and life? Is there really a problem with more schooling as the perceived objective for students during middle and high school? At this stage in their lives, do they need to be aware of any more exalted purpose for what they are doing? And the concept that schooling gets you ahead in life hardly seems a bad incentive for students of any age or social background.

Schooling for more schooling's sake is, in fact, problematic as an answer to the question "why go to school?" It provides an ultimately unsatisfactory answer to the question of how school connects to life. Students can be told that education eventually leads to material wealth and status and perhaps become convinced that this is so, even when their ideas are as fragmentary as the ones we sampled here. The problem, however, is that the relation is solely an instrumental one: Investment and outcome—means and end—bear only an arbitrary connection. No reason is apparent as to why educational pursuits should be the object of society's approval and reward.

In this case, then, the value of intellectual activity derives solely from its role in a means-end relationship that is arbitrary. No intrinsic connection exists between activity and outcome. And here lies the downside. Once an

Box 2.1

HOW STUDENTS REGARD THE VALUE OF SCHOOL

Question: Are the things you are learning in school going to be of any value to you once you've finished your schooling?

Responses from Best-Practice-School Students*

NO VALUE (40 PERCENT)
- Many things, especially in history and math, will never be used and are a waste of time.
- Most of the things we learn in school are not important and will not be important later in life. Most of the stuff will be forgotten.
- Only if you want to have facts to make yourself look good in a conversation. Like the Ming dynasty we're studying in history now. Why else would you need to know this?

VALUE FOR COLLEGE (35 PERCENT)
- Learning to make deadlines and manage my time will stay with me throughout college.
- School gives you a small taste of everything and allows you to choose something when you go to college.
- What would you do without an education? Obviously that's the key to college and then our career.

VALUE FOR SPECIFIC CAREERS (15 PERCENT)
- Math, if you want a career in math, like money management
- You need to know about our history if you're going into politics.

PERSONAL TRAITS, SKILLS (35 PERCENT)
- Learning to communicate
- Learning to interact with other individuals and developing confidence
- Acquiring a work ethic and learning how to work with other people
- Learning to formulate ideas and be able to present them articulately

* Percentages do not total 100 since some students offered responses in more than one category.

Responses from Struggling-School Students

NON-SPECIFIC VALUE (50 PERCENT)
- Helps you get somewhere in life. Without education you can't get anywhere.
- Helps you to be a better person, not hang out on the street. Sets people on the right track.

- What you learn in school determines what you can do in the future. Certain jobs require certain knowledge.
- You need a good education to get into a good college or get a good job.

VALUE FOR SPECIFIC CAREERS (50 PERCENT)
- Math skills look good on my resume and would help me be an accountant.
- Math would help you start a business organization.
- History would be good if you want to be a teacher.
- It depends what work you're going to do. If you're good in Spanish you can be a translator.

activity becomes identified as merely a means to an end, it tends to be devalued as unimportant in its own right. It is engaged in only because it is believed to produce a future dividend that is valued. The risk then looms large that, sooner or later, one may become skeptical of this connection, at which point the activity loses its purpose.

The value of an intrinsically valued activity, in contrast, lies in the activity itself. The benefits of the activity emanate directly from it. People engage in it because it is experienced as valuable in its own right. The advantage is clear: Continued commitment to the activity is ensured. It is not dependent on a relation between the activity and some independently valued outcome.

Activities that have clear, readily discernible intrinsic value thus provide the firmest basis for sustaining intellectual motivation through childhood and adolescence and into adulthood. Students experience for themselves the value of the activities they engage in and develop commitment to them as a way of doing things. They are able to make use of them for their own purposes, and they see the fruits of their labors. They know what they are doing and why. This characterization begins to sound like the outcome every educator hopes for—students who have acquired the skills and disposition to be independent, self-directed learners.

There is less consensus regarding the next question—how to make such a vision a reality. It is not achieved by exhortation—by telling students that certain kinds of activities are valuable, or even how or why they are valuable. Instead, adults' most important role is to introduce students to the kinds of intellectual activities that have a value that becomes evident in the course of engaging them and developing the skills they entail. Students must discover this value for themselves; but by serving as guides and coaches as students engage such an activity, adults model both their own commitment to the activity and a belief in its worth.

Quite simply, then, it matters a great deal what kinds of things we ask young students to do in school, with the consequences potentially very long-range ones. We have a window of opportunity of only a few brief years during which students will decide whether the things we ask them to do in school are worthwhile. Their reaching a negative conclusion ought not to be risked. We can eliminate the risk by ensuring the activities we choose have a clearly visible purpose that makes sense to students.

Inquiry and argument are these kinds of activities. Students readily experience and appreciate their value as they engage in them and gain mastery of the skills they entail. They are empowering. Once they are found useful in pursuing individual and collective goals, no further incentive is needed for practicing and perfecting the skills they entail.

The Challenge of Meritocracy

Would intellectual skills such as inquiry and argument develop on their own if we simply allowed children the freedom to pursue their own interests, independent of adult guidance? The answer is probably no, according to the evidence I present in later chapters. Yet inquiry is often described as a "natural" activity of the preschool years. Children are naturally curious, it is said, and eager to explore the world around them. The activity is its own reward—no other incentive is needed. By middle childhood, however, this "natural curiosity" appears to go underground in most children.

What causes this change, and is the school system responsible? Critics such as Nicholls (1989) reply to the second question with an emphatic yes. A concern about whether they are "good at something" begins to eclipse interest in the thing itself, and children want to invest themselves in only those activities in which they see themselves as high performers in comparison to others. By the middle-school years, Nicholls claims, children have adopted this ego-involvement stance toward school in which they approach and evaluate every activity by comparing their own performance to that of others. The quality of the child's involvement changes from a focus on the task, and his or her own relationship to it, to a state of ego involvement in which the focus is on the child's standing relative to others. Success is equated with superiority over others.

Research by Dweck and colleagues (Dweck and Leggett, 1988) has shown that this difference in orientation affects performance on cognitive tasks. Low self-evaluation with respect to an activity diminishes effort: "Why keep trying if I'm no good at this?" Related to these beliefs are shifting conceptions of the causes of competence, from one of effortful accomplishment (in early childhood), to one of fixed capacity, with a consequent devaluing of effort: "I know I'll never get any better." Dweck finds individual differences among children in these beliefs; but the developmental trend, if any, is toward greater belief in ability as a fixed entity with increasing age (Kinlaw and Kurtz-Costes, 2003). Adolescents, Nicholls (1989) reports, are less likely than children to value effortful over effortless accomplishment.

Nicholls (1989) further argues that schools serve as models of a competitive, meritocratic society in which individual differences in accomplishment are reflected in status and material reward. In this sense, schools are well suited for socializing children into such a society, serving as vehicles to focus children's attention on evaluating their activities not in terms of intrinsic value but in terms of their performance in these activities relative to the performance of others. The concept of an individual's "investment in education" takes on the meaning of investment in skills that will increase the individual's relative standing rather than yield anything of intrinsic value. Potential dropouts are encouraged not to leave school because of the negative effect on their future social status and material well-being. Rarely does the suggestion arise that in leaving school students might be missing anything of intrinsic value.

The pressures of a meritocratic, competitive society are not ones that schools can erase or ignore. The challenge of educating children in a meritocracy, then, becomes one of maintaining a child's interest and motivation to engage in varied pursuits, in the face of increasingly apparent individual differences in talent, skill, and achievement, and the inevitable increasing social emphasis these differences receive. To the extent the intellectual activities that students are asked to engage in are ones with intrinsic value and power that are readily apparent, the goal of maintaining motivation to engage in them for their own sake begins to appear more within reach.

Again, then, it is crucial for educators to choose instructional activities with great thought and care. If students are to embrace these activities as worth the effort they entail, their value must quickly become evident. "These are powerful tools that can help you to pursue your goals," the coach/teacher who guides the activities seeks to convey to students, "rather than occasions for assessment of your competence relative to others, as part of an endless ranking enterprise."

Intangible messages like these are difficult for a teacher to convey to students, and such messages are conveyed less by telling than by modeling and example. For there to be any hope of success, teachers must have earned a significant degree of trust from their students. "If you pay attention and get involved, you'll see that what I'm asking you to do is worth doing," the teacher in effect says. "You'll see the value yourself if you try it. I wouldn't waste your time with it if it weren't so." If the message is to succeed, students must see themselves and their teachers as players on the same team, exactly the characteristic we saw so sadly missing at the struggling school.

Reaching beyond the mindset of meritocracy to embrace the intrinsic value of intellectual engagement is no less a challenge for the more privileged students of the best-practice school. The intense pressure to excel academically is so great that competition inevitably becomes fierce. Each day affords new opportunities to ask, "Where do I stand relative to others?" The competitive mindset overtakes interest: "I must like and pursue what I am good at, so I can get even better at it, maybe even better than anyone else." In this climate, it is a challenge indeed to seek and to find the intrinsic value in any activity.

For all students, the window of opportunity open to teachers to influence formation of such values may be a brief one, likely to close by the end of the middle-school years. Teachers must capitalize on the opportunity to secure students' trust that they are working together on the same team. And teachers must then honor that trust by engaging students in activities that students will readily be able to see for themselves are worth doing. In time, with continuing teamwork, students will come to value the intellectual skills they develop in these activities as ones worth having.

Epistemological Foundations of Intellectual Values

We have focused thus far largely on the obstacles to students' development of intellectual values—to their seeing intellectual engagement as intrinsically worthwhile in its own right. We turn now to what might develop on the positive side, as a foundation for the emergence and consolidation of strong and secure intellectual values. The answer I propose is that students' understandings of what it means to learn and to know are a key part of this foundation.

The study of students' developing epistemological understanding has blossomed in the last decade (see Hofer and Pintrich, 1997, 2002, for review), with the result that we now have a fairly convergent picture of a series of steps that mark development toward more mature epistemological understanding in the years from early childhood to early adulthood (Table 2.1).

Preschool-aged children are *realists*. They regard what one knows as an immediate reading of what is out there. Beliefs are faithful copies of reality. They are received directly from the external world, rather than constructed

Table 2.1. Steps toward mature epistemological understanding

Level	Assertions are . . .	Knowledge is . . .	Critical thinking is . . .
Realist	Copies of an external reality	From an external source; certain	Unnecessary
Absolutist	Facts that are correct or incorrect in their representation of reality	From an external source; certain but not directly accessible, producing false beliefs	A vehicle for comparing assertions to reality and determining their truth or falsehood.
Multiplist	Opinions freely chosen by and accountable only to their owners	Generated by human minds; uncertain	Irrelevant
Evaluativist	Judgments that can be evaluated and compared according to criteria of argument and evidence	Generated by human minds; uncertain but susceptible to evaluation	Valued as a vehicle that promotes sound assertions and enhances understanding

by the knower. Hence, there are no inaccurate renderings of events, nor any possibility of conflicting beliefs, because everyone perceives the same external reality.

Not until about age four does a knower begin to emerge in a child's conceptions of knowing. Children become aware that mental representations, as products of the human mind, do not necessarily duplicate external reality. Before children achieve a concept of false belief, they are unwilling to attribute to another person a belief that they themselves know to be false (Perner, 1991). Once they attain this conception, the knower—and knowledge as mental representations produced by knowers—comes to life.

The products of knowing, however, are still more firmly attached to the known object than to the knower. Hence, while inadequate or incorrect information can produce false beliefs, they are easily correctable by reference to an external reality—the known object. If you and I disagree, one of us is right and one is wrong and resolving the matter is simply a matter of finding out which is which. At this *absolutist* level of epistemological understanding, knowledge is regarded as an accumulating set of certain facts (see Table 2.1).

Further progress in epistemological understanding can be characterized as an extended task of coordinating the subjective and the objective elements of knowing (Kuhn, Cheney, and Weinstock, 2000). At the realist and absolutist levels, the objective dominates. By adolescence a radical change in epistemological understanding is likely to emerge. In a word, everyone now becomes right. The discovery that reasonable people—even experts—disagree is the likely source of adolescents recognizing the uncertain, subjective aspect of knowing. This recognition initially assumes such proportions, however, that it eclipses recognition of any objective standard that could serve as a basis for evaluating conflicting claims. Adolescents typically fall into "a poisoned well of doubt" (Chandler and Lalonde, 2003), and they fall hard and deep. At this *multiplist* (sometimes called *relativist*) level of epistemological understanding, knowledge consists not of facts but of opinions, freely chosen by their holders as personal possessions and accordingly not open to challenge.

Knowledge is now clearly seen as emanating from the knower, rather than the known, but at the significant cost of any discriminability among competing knowledge claims. That ubiquitous slogan of adolescence—"whatever"—holds sway. The multiplist may come to equate lack of discriminability with tolerance. Because everyone has a right to their opinion, all opinions are equally right.

Hoisting oneself out of the "whatever" well of multiplicity and indiscriminability is much harder than the quick and easy fall into its depths. By adulthood, many, though by no means all, adolescents will have reintegrated the objective dimension of knowing and achieved the understanding that, while everyone has a right to their opinion, some opinions are in fact more right than others, to the extent they are better supported by argument and evidence. Justification for a belief becomes more than personal preference. "Whatever" is no longer the automatic response to any assertion—there are legitimate discriminations and choices to be made. Rather than facts or opinions, knowledge at this *evaluativist* level of epistemological understanding consists of judgments, which require support in a framework of alternatives, evidence, and argument.

This cognitive evolution cannot by itself yield the valuing of intellectual engagement that is our concern in this chapter. But it does provide an essential foundation for its development. Adolescents who never progress beyond the absolutist belief in certain knowledge, or the multiplist's equation of knowledge with personal preference, lack a reason to engage in sustained intellectual inquiry. If facts can be ascertained with certainty and are readily available to anyone who seeks them, as the absolutist understands, or if any claim is as valid as any other, as the multiplist understands, there is little point to expending the mental effort that the evaluation of claims entails.

Table 2.2. Intellectual values and levels of epistemological understanding

	Struggling-school middle-school students (%)	Best-practice-school middle-school students (%)	Best-practice-school high-school students (%)	Best-practice-school parents (%)
Valuing inquiry	10	36	—	—
Valuing debate	14	40	52	77
Evaluativist epistemological understanding	33	60	70	82

Note. Respondents categorized as "evaluativist" responded to a majority of items in an evaluativist pattern. Those categorized as "valuing debate" responded "disagree" to all three items and those categorized as "valuing inquiry" responded "disagree" to the inquiry item.

Four items were used to assess epistemological beliefs across several domains. In each, two conflicting views were identified, for example, "Robin thinks the first piece of music they listen to is better and Chris thinks the second piece of music they listen to is better." The respondent is asked, "Can only one of their views be right, or could both have some rightness?" If the response is that both could have some rightness, a second question is asked, "Could one view be better or more right than the other?" An evaluativist pattern of response is identified as a "both" answer to the first question and a positive answer to the second. A multiplist pattern consists of a "both" answer to the first question but a negative response to the second, and an absolutist pattern consists of a positive answer to the first question.

Only at the evaluativist level are thinking and reason recognized as essential support for beliefs and actions. Thinking is the process that enables us to make informed choices between conflicting claims. Understanding this leads a person to value thinking and to be willing to expend the effort that it entails (see Table 2.1).

Epistemological Understanding and Intellectual Values of Students

Have the different backgrounds and school experiences of students from the best-practice and struggling schools led to identifiable differences in their intellectual values and levels of epistemological understanding? To answer this question, we administered measures of both constructs to students from each school—twenty-five sixth through eighth graders at the best-practice school and twenty-one eighth graders at the struggling school. The results are summarized in Table 2.2.

The instrument used to assess level of epistemological understanding is adapted from research by Kuhn, Cheney, and Weinstock (2000). The question used to assess the valuing of intellectual inquiry is the following:

People usually have pretty good ideas about things. They can try to go out and get more information, but they'll probably find out that the ideas they started out with were the best ones. Do you strongly agree, sort of agree, or disagree? If you disagree, what do you think?

Following is one of the three questions used to assess the valuing of intellectual argument and debate:

Many social issues, like the death penalty, gun control, or medical care, are pretty much matters of personal opinion, and there is no basis for saying that one person's opinion is any better than another's. So there's not much point in people having discussions about these kinds of issues. Do you strongly agree, sort of agree, or disagree? If you disagree, what do you think?

Topics of two other parallel questions are political candidates (suggested to be not worth discussing because choices are a matter of personal preference) and world peace (suggested to be not worth discussing because the problem is too difficult to solve). Note that all of the valuing questions are presented in an inverted direction. The respondent cannot be judged as displaying intellectual values simply by agreeing with a presented statement. Rather, respondents must disagree with the statement and indicate why. Reasons individuals offered for disagreement with the statement included the alleged value of discussion in enhancing individual or collective understanding, solving problems, and resolving conflicts.

As reflected in Table 2.2, middle-school students at the struggling school were unlikely to see either inquiry or debate as valuable—not a great surprise. There is not much point in talking about issues or getting more information, they largely agreed. Percentages for middle-school students at the best-practice school were higher; but, still, less than half voiced consistent commitment to inquiry or debate as valued activities. Students at the best-practice school were more likely, however, to have reached the evaluativist epistemological understanding that there may be no single right answer, but some answers are nonetheless more right than others.

Can we anticipate that these students' epistemological understanding and intellectual values will continue to develop as they progress through adolescence and into adulthood? We were fortunate in being able to secure responses to these same questions from twenty-seven high-school students and fifty-six parents at the best-practice school (see Table 2.2). It was not possible to interview equivalent groups at the struggling school, a difference reflective of the striking overall difference between the two populations. Best-practice families were interested to learn about our research, happy to participate, and eager to find out the results.

Best-practice high-schoolers, as seen in Table 2.2, show an even higher level on each dimension than do their middle-school peers, and parents of these students show an even higher level still. It is clear, then, that these middle-schoolers belong to a subculture in which such values are the norm and they are highly likely to come to espouse them themselves.

It does not follow, however, that these privileged young adolescents see their schoolwork as having much to do with the intrinsic, in contrast to the instrumental, value of intellectual investment. Herein, then, lies the challenge for those who teach them—to establish and strengthen the link between intellectual engagement and the work they are asked to do at school. These students, perhaps more than anything else, need help in finding some genuine purpose within the context of their busy school lives. I return to these concerns in the concluding chapter.

Nurturing Intellectual Values

Children are engaged in an extended sense-making endeavor, and school is likely to be the first major social institution that they are forced to make sense of while still at a tender age. We would like to think of schools as a support, rather than as a challenge, in children's sense-making efforts. We would also like to think of schools as settings that introduce students to intellectual engagement and its value—to the life of the mind. Yet in the end it is the child who must construct meaning and who will make the choices and commitments that follow.

We can, however, provide a nurturing environment for the values and skills we hope to see develop. One way to support the development of intellectual values is to do all we can to make sure that the requisite foundation of epistemological understanding develops. The transitions from realist to absolutist to multiplist portrayed in Table 2.1 do not require a great deal of tending. Unless the child's experience is unusually restricted, children become aware that people's beliefs differ and they must figure out a way of understanding this state of affairs. The vast majority take at least a brief dip, and more often a prolonged one, into the well of multiplicity. The transition from multiplist to evaluativist, however, is another story. It is helping young people climb out of the multiplist well that requires the concerted attention of parents and educators, especially as it is this progression that is critical to the development of intellectual values.

Intellectual values, we have said, cannot be instilled by exhortation—by telling students that a particular kind of activity is valuable, or even how or why it is valuable. Only their own experiences can lead them to the conviction that inquiry and reasoned argument offer the most promising path to deciding between competing claims, resolving conflicts, solving problems, and achieving goals. The more fruitful adult role is that of introducing young people to activities that have a value that becomes self-evident as the youths engage them and develop the skills they entail. An essential aspect of the adult's role is conveying his or her belief in the value of the activity and commitment to it. As students' skill and commitment and self-direction increase, the adult's role fades.

As the classroom observations described in this book document, the activities we engage students in at school typically do not have these characteristics. It is thus crucial to introduce activities that do have this intrinsic worth and to make this worth apparent by engaging students in their practice, thereby enabling the students to observe their value for themselves. In the two middle sections of the book, we examine two broad families of skills that have these characteristics—the skills of inquiry, examined in Part II, and the skills of argument, examined in Part III.

INQUIRY ┃ II

Developing inquiry skills is not an educational mission we need to work hard to sell. As the mission statements sampled in Chapter 1 reflect, schools all want their students to acquire the skills that will equip them to become independent learners, able to seek answers to their own questions. Education theorists today (Eisenhart, Finkel, and Marion, 1996; Brown, 1997; de Jong and van Joolingen, 1998; Bransford, Brown, and Cocking, 1999; McGinn and Roth, 1999) are equally supportive of inquiry as an educational goal. Inquiry learning, they claim, is superior to traditional instruction because it involves students in authentic investigation of real phenomena, in the process fostering intellectual skills like those practiced by professional scientists in generating new knowledge. Growing enthusiasm for inquiry learning has paralleled the growth of the educational technology field, and the result has been development of a wide variety of educational software and project-based curricula designed to engage students in inquiry, some of which we examine in this chapter.

Inquiry curricula are not focused on the particular knowledge students may acquire. Teachers would be unlikely to teach information included on state tests via an inquiry method. Instead, the primary goal of an inquiry curriculum is to teach students how to inquire and learn. If achieved, the outcome appears to be a powerful one, well worth the effort invested. Students become equipped to take charge of their own learning, choosing the questions they wish to investigate and seeking and finding answers to them.

Two characteristics are striking about the inquiry learning movement. The first is how widely it has been embraced. Almost any middle-school teacher will agree that developing inquiry or "research" skills is important and will probably be aware of their prominence in district, state, or national standards. And most—including Ms. B from the struggling school and Mrs. O from the best-practice school—proclaim these skills to be among their own objectives. The second striking characteristic is how little teachers have to go on in striving to fulfill these objectives. What, exactly, are the skills that need to be developed and how do teachers ensure their students are making progress toward acquiring them?

What Are Inquiry Skills?

Compare a teacher's position in seeking to develop students' inquiry skills versus their literacy or mathematical skills. In the latter case, the teacher can draw on a plethora of finely calibrated assessment instruments that have been widely accepted as identifying a student's level of achievement with great accuracy—a student's reading level is routinely identified, for example, as year six, month five. Classroom teachers are not only able but in fact usually required to undertake frequent assessments of these skill levels, and evaluations of the teacher's own performance are influenced by the results. There is little ambiguity here about what students have or have not achieved. Nor is there any scarcity of curriculum materials designed to promote this achievement.

Inquiry skills, in contrast, lack even a clear subject area. Most often, inquiry skills are regarded as part of science education, and virtually all current curriculum standards in science education include inquiry skills. But inquiry skills are also commonly found as curriculum goals in Social Studies and even in language arts (e.g., Levstik and Barton, 2001, p. xi). Yet even in science, where they are most prevalent, these goals and standards remain couched in the most general of terms. The National Science Education Standards (National Research Council, 1996), for example, identify these skills as goals of inquiry learning for fifth through eighth grades:

Identify questions that can be answered through scientific investigations
Design and conduct a scientific investigation
Use appropriate tools and techniques to gather, analyze, and interpret data
Develop descriptions, explanations, predictions, and models using evidence
Think critically and logically to make the relationships between evidence and explanations.

Some elaboration is provided under each of these standards. For example, under "design and conduct a scientific investigation," subskills identified include "systematic observation, making accurate measurements, and identifying and controlling variables." A guide for teachers published by the National Research Council (2000) as a supplement to the standards notes that students commonly have difficulty performing these various skills (pp. 78–79), but the guide offers no further insight into the nature of the skills, the nature of students' difficulties in performing them, or the processes by which they can be acquired.

How, then, do science teachers undertake to develop students' inquiry skills? Unless they attend a professional development workshop tailored to this purpose, most are likely to begin by consulting a sourcebook of suggested activities (with convenient "equipment needed" lists for each). Such guides, however, typically say little about what students are likely to do when engaged in these activities. What should teachers expect and look for? Most important, what do the skills look like that they should be trying to promote, and how can the teacher determine whether students are on track in developing them?

Even the most conscientious and informed teachers are left with little to go on. A vast, seemingly uncharted terrain remains between executing the activity and developing the skills. How does a teacher help a student to "analyze and interpret data" or to "think critically and logically to make the relationships between evidence and explanations"? What teachers have to settle for is assessment of the activities themselves rather than the skills that students do or do not display in engaging them. If an activity seems a "rich" one—that is, one that students maintain sustained involvement in over a period of time without losing interest—then it is deemed an inquiry activity successful for the age group. But even in these relatively favorable circumstances, teachers would be hard-pressed to identify just what skills the students are acquiring or to document their progress.

What, then, in fact goes on in today's middle-school classrooms in the name of inquiry learning? How effective are such efforts and how might they become more effective? These are the major questions this chapter asks. We again focus on observations of the Social Studies classrooms in the struggling school and best-practice school introduced in Chapter 2. Here I introduce the teacher's perspective. What was her agenda, in particular with respect to teaching the intellectual skills of inquiry? And how did students respond? What did they appear to accomplish?

Given the very different atmospheres of the two schools, I was surprised to find that the activities Ms. B and Mrs. O engaged their students in were not as different from one another as I anticipated they might be, even though the students' skill levels and the way they engaged the activities were markedly different. Moreover, the two teachers spoke about their objectives in similar terms. Both emphasized the importance of skill development—in particular, skills they expected their students would need in high school. These skills included the ability to gain information effectively from text but also "research" skills, which they both took to mean the ability to obtain information independently. How, then, did the two teachers go about developing these skills in their students, and what were the apparent results of their efforts?

Developing Inquiry Skills at the Struggling School

I began observing Ms. B's eighth-grade Social Studies class at the time they were beginning a new unit on the nations of the world with a particular focus on the United Nations and its role in international relations. In their initial homework assignment, the students were asked to listen to BBC World News (which they could access through the Internet in the computer lab after school) and find out about the U.N. and its purpose. Because they lived in New York City, most students had at least some awareness of the existence of the U.N. building and the connection of the U.N. to international relations. Ms. B further explained that each student would choose a member country and serve as a representative of that country at the U.N. To do a good job as a representative, they would need to research their country and they would be required to present the results of their research in a three-page paper due in several weeks.

While Ms. B was presenting the assignment to the class as a group, she struggled to maintain order, as she did, I observed, whenever she spoke to the class as a whole for any longer than two or three minutes. Ms. B's effort to maintain enough control so she could be heard consisted of raising her hands to shoulder level and repeating "Sshh!" softly several times. This reduced the noise level noticeably, but only briefly; and when it again reached a certain threshold, Ms. B would repeat this gesture. At any one time, at most two-thirds of the class were attending to her, and often less than half. Some students were silent but looking elsewhere in the room, writing, or looking at something on their desk, and at least some were always engaged in conversation.

At the next class period, Ms. B had planned to take the class to the library, where they would choose their countries and begin their research. She announced this plan at the beginning of class, once students were seated. The trip to the library, one floor below, required the same lining-up procedure in the corridor at the points of departure and arrival described in Chapter 2. By the time students were seated in the library, only twenty-five minutes of the class period remained.

The first item on Ms. B's agenda was to collect the homework assignment about the U.N. Only nine of thirty students had anything to turn in. Ms. B expressed her reaction openly: "I feel very frustrated right now, because we can't go ahead if you haven't done the homework." Students seemed un-concerned. Most were enjoying the opportunity for socialization that the close quarters of the library allowed. (They were seated around large tables, rather than in front-facing desks as in their classroom.) After a noisy few moments, Ms. B got the class's attention and announced what she later confirmed was a spontaneous decision: "Those of you who have done the homework, come sit down at this table and we will get to work. I'm going to work with the people who have come prepared. I can't work with the rest of you on this assignment if you haven't completed the homework."

After another few moments, the nine students who had completed their homework were seated around one table with Ms. B. The other twenty-one students remained at another table. No books or papers were out, and there was no pretense of their being engaged in anything but social interaction, which they continued until the bell rang fifteen minutes later. During this time, they were ignored by Ms. B and by the librarian, who was also present.

At Ms. B's table, she showed students a set of index cards she had pre-pared, each with the name of a country on it, one for each member of the class. She told students that they would be allowed to look through the set and choose a country to represent. Students showed some interest in this activity, but the country names appeared to mean little to them and they chose seemingly randomly, in some cases with prompting from Ms. B.

In the class I observed the following week, students were scheduled to go to the computer lab to do research on their countries using the Internet. All of the students had by then been assigned a country, and they also had been given an assignment sheet containing guiding questions. In addition to questions covering factual information about the country, the sheet in-cluded several questions about the country's role in the U.N. and its stance with respect to human rights. The questions on this sheet, Ms. B explained, would help them to prepare the reports on their countries that were due the next week.

A computer with Internet access was available for each student. Students had been instructed in computer and Internet use in their computer class, and they all sat down and accessed the Internet on their computers without assistance. During the remainder of the period, Ms. B and I circulated around the room, I merely observing and Ms. B observing and occasionally offering suggestions. Ms. B tended to work with a single student at a time for five or six minutes; and during the middle of the period, she disappeared from the room for about ten minutes, so she ended up speaking with a total of only three or four students.

During the thirty or so minutes of class time, I observed about half of the students engaged in off-task activity. Ms. B did not acknowledge these students. Many of them accessed Internet sites that had nothing to do with their assigned country or accessed other computer software such as a drawing program, while others merely talked to one another and ignored their computers.

The remaining fifteen or so students who engaged in activity related to the assignment immediately went to one of the search engines they seemed well acquainted with, such as Yahoo or Ask Jeeves. The latter allows users to type a question, and the program then displays material associated with that question. Following are the questions related to human rights that I observed two students ask the program:

What rights do people have in Germany?
South Korea, do they abuse people there?

Other students simply typed in the name of their country. Whether a student took this approach or attempted to formulate a more specific question, however, appeared not to make a great deal of difference. In either case, the search results comprised passages of text of varying lengths from one paragraph to several pages. In no case did I observe a student attempting to read this text or make notes from it, beyond confirming that it made reference to their assigned country. Once this was confirmed, a single goal emerged—to print the text. The computer lab had only one printer, networked to all the computers, so a queue soon formed at the printer as students waited to print the material from their computers, and the printer area became a social hub.

Near the end of the period, Ms. B had returned to class and observed the activity at the printer. She instructed all students to return to their seats and said the following:

> You are not working well. We're going to log off and never come to the computer lab again. You're not supposed to print entire web sites. You should take notes in a computer file or a notebook. You've abused the privilege of coming here.

Ms. B went on in this vein for several minutes, naming particular offenders and instructing them to see her after class for further reprimand. She then said to the class as a whole, "You have five more minutes for research, until the end of the period." During this remaining five minutes, Ms. B continued her discussions with individual students; and during this time, I observed not a single student make any motion to return to his or her computer. Instead, they sat with bags packed waiting for the bell to ring.

Ms. B allowed me to look at the reports that students turned in the following week, and I was surprised that most of them had managed to compile two or three pages of text about the country they had been assigned. The text rarely went beyond encyclopedia-level general information about the country and clearly had been pasted together from whatever sources the student had found—mostly, I suspected, in a form that remained largely undigested by the student.

During the next two weeks, Ms. B introduced several further activities related to national governments, international relations, and the U.N. The major one, an essay and subsequent debate on whether the U.N. should be abolished, is described in Chapter 6. The other two involved asking students to devise a fictitious country. In one activity, they were asked to design a flag for the country and in the other to design a currency. Each assignment included associated questions designed to probe students' thinking about governments. The flag assignment included giving the country a name and developing its "mission statement." The currency assignment went beyond design to ask these questions:

1. How will money be distributed in your country? Who will receive it?
2. How will you guarantee that money flows back into your country?
3. What economy type does your method of distribution resemble—socialism, capitalism, or communism? (These terms had been introduced earlier in the semester.)

In both these in-class assignments, the attention and interest of students not engaged in off-task activity was absorbed entirely by the artistic aspects of the assignment—designing the flags and currency and using colored pencils to color them—and in the class period allotted for each, only a few students went on to the questions at the bottom of the assignment sheet. At the end of the class period, I was surprised to hear Ms. B make these concluding remarks to the class:

> Today you had to spend a lot of time thinking about the economy. I'm proud you recognized that dividing money equally is not necessarily best for your country. Even distribution isn't necessarily fair distribution.

My own reactions to my observations in Ms. B's classroom ranged from admiration to dismay, with a number of sentiments in between. I was impressed that Ms. B, a young woman with only a few years' teaching experience working under very adverse conditions, had engaged her students in the range and variety of activities that she had. She could have gotten by with much less, with more pedestrian assignments of reading textbooks and answering questions at the ends of chapters. The impression I got from talk-

Box 3.1

CHART OUTLINING THE RESEARCH PROCESS IN MS. B'S CLASSROOM

Inquiry: Ask questions [inquire] about your topic/subject

Gathering information:
  Interviews
  Surveys
  Graphs and tables
  Information and reference books
  Internet

Compile research into a written rough draft

Organize into chronological sequence:
  Introduction
  Facts and details
  Conclusion

Revise and edit

ing with Ms. B was that it was critical to her to believe that she was teaching something meaningful in the midst of these difficult conditions. She would not have been satisfied with getting by; that approach did not fit her self-image. She had a firm sense of "research skills" as something she believed her students should learn and she was doing her best to provide experiences to develop these skills. Indeed, the chart in Box 3.1 was displayed prominently in her classroom. After it was introduced to students as a guide for their research activities and the research reports they would write, it remained on the classroom wall through the rest of the semester.

Ms. B clearly believed that the activities she engaged her students in, and particularly the research paper, were involving them in inquiry activities. Her goals and intentions in this respect were not in question. It seems less likely, however, that she had a realistic sense of the effectiveness of her efforts in realizing these intentions. In order to maintain her positive sense of what she was doing, I concluded, Ms. B needed to distance herself from a lot of what was going on in her classroom, even to the literal extent of leaving the classroom for brief periods. She adaptively lowered her standards such that it was not necessary that all students be engaged in order for her to proceed with her agenda. Involvement of even a minority of the class (as in the occasion in the library) would suffice. At times, however, she seemed to deliberately shield herself from the reality of what students were doing as they engaged independently in an assignment—for example, the flags or currency assignment. In these cases, the reality was plain to see, and it seemed she was choosing to ignore it.

Did Ms. B have a realistic sense of the skill levels and capabilities of her students? In their major research assignment, I was struck by the enormous gap between what Ms. B was asking them to do and their ability to do it. The Internet is widely admired as a vast new resource for students, but their ability to extract meaning from electronic text and make use of it is no different from their ability to do so from conventional text. Students through the ages have complied with assignments asking them to locate information in a reference source and submit it in the format of a research report. The Internet makes the search more convenient but otherwise does not change the task.

A different set of skills is entailed in authentic inquiry, skills that require comprehension and communication abilities but cannot be reduced to them. These skills are not intuitively given. Both in this and the next chapters, I explore what these skills are and how a roadmap of their development might be of value to the middle-school classroom teacher. First, however, let us examine what goes on in the name of inquiry in a Social Studies class at the best-practice school.

Developing Inquiry Skills at the Best-Practice School

During roughly the same period of weeks that I observed Ms. B's eighth-grade Social Studies class at the struggling school, I observed Mrs. O's seventh-grade Social Studies class at the best-practice school. The class was engaged in the study of American history, in particular, colonial life prior to the Revolutionary War.

Sixth grade at the best-practice school is considered a transitional year into the middle school, while seventh grade is when development of the academic skills critical to high school becomes a priority. Grade 7 American history course content is dictated by district and state standards as part of a carefully coordinated K-12 sequence; students take another year-long course in this subject in high school. Mrs. O indicated she saw this year as one in which she could focus on the skill development that would prepare students for the rigors of the more advanced coursework they would encounter in high school and beyond.

She identified these skills as accessing and processing significant amounts

Box 3.2

WRITING ASSIGNMENT GUIDE IN MRS. O'S CLASS

Thesis: When the Native Americans and the Europeans met, both cultures changed though the Native Americans experienced the greater change.

Paragraph 1 topic sentence: The culture of the Europeans changed after coming into contact with the Native Americans.

- Explanation: Explain WHY this change happened.
- 1st main category: Explain one general reason why the Europeans changed.
- Details: This is your proof. Use descriptive details to explain the change. DO NOT LIST. Be specific as to which group was affected. Prove the category point.
- 2nd main category: Explain another general reason why they changed.
- Details: This is your proof. Use descriptive details to explain the change. DO NOT LIST. Be specific as to which group was affected. Prove the category point.
- 3rd main category: Optional

Paragraph 2 topic sentence: The lives of the Native Americans were changed even more after coming in contact with the Europeans.

- Explanation: Explain WHY this change happened.
- 1st main category: Explain one general reason why the Native Americans changed.
- Details: This is your proof. Use descriptive details to explain the change. DO NOT LIST. Be specific as to which group was affected. Prove the category point.
- 2nd main category: Explain another general reason why the Native Americans changed.
- Details: This is your proof. Use descriptive details to explain the change. DO NOT LIST. Be specific as to which group was affected. Prove the category point.
- 3rd main category: Optional

WARNING: DO *NOT* JUST LIST THE DETAILS.

of detailed information; organizing it into themes and relationships, such as cause and effect; and learning how to present it in a thesis-and-support structure, as detailed in the template shown in Box 3.2, which she presented to students as a tool. As a result, Mrs. O's course covered an extraordinary amount of detailed content, which she expected students to organize and retain and be able to present in appropriate ways in the many assignments and tests she gave. Mrs. O's reputation was one of a committed but demanding teacher who had very high expectations for students. The Social Studies course had the reputation of being the most difficult one in the seventh-grade curriculum. Students said the volume of work and time required to do it was much greater than in any of their other courses, and Social Studies was the course in which the largest percentage of seventh graders (about 10 percent) received skills center or resource room help.

Students for the most part accepted these expectations and worked hard to fulfill them. Daily homework assignments and frequent tests served as the explicit structure of the course. During the months I observed, the class was studying five different colonial settlements, and each had its own lettered set of materials. Students kept large notebooks in which they were required to organize all material related to a particular topic. These included notes from readings, notes from class, maps and other class handouts, review sheets, quizzes, and exams. Assignment K, for example, covered the New England colonies. Box 3.3 displays the assignment sheet for Assignment K, indicating the topics, questions to be answered under each topic, and the source materials to be consulted. There was also a reading assignment from the course textbook (*The American Nation,* published in 2000 and replacing the earlier text *A History of the Republic,* both published by Prentice-Hall). Here is the homework assignment given as part of assignment K:

Main idea #1: Religion influenced the way of life

1. Lived together in a town. Describe one. Explain why.
2. Sunday was a serious day. Explain how and why.
3. Had town meetings. Describe one. Why were they able to use this form of government?
4. Describe their belief about work.
5. Educations laws passed in 1647. List. Why were they passed?

Main idea #2: New England geography influenced the way of life

1. Soil. Economy?
2. Forests. Economy?
3. Ocean. Economy?

Mrs. O made explicit to students and stressed the importance of the skills they were acquiring. To help develop these skills, she told me, she collected students' notes from their reading and their required review sheets and

Box 3.3

ASSIGNMENT K IN MRS. O'S CLASS

SOURCE 1. TOPOGRAPHY MAP
Describe the features of the topography of New England.
Describe the coastline from Boston up into Maine.
Describe the relative location of Boston.

SOURCES 2 & 3. MAPS OF MASSACHUSETTS BAY AND BOSTON
Count the number of harbors that you see.
Make an observation about the settlements in Massachusetts Bay colony.

SOURCE 4. MAP OF NEW ENGLAND
Describe the typical settlement pattern of New England.
Trace the river that cuts Connecticut and Massachusetts in half. What is its
    name? What colony is to the east of it above Massachusetts? What is the
    situation with the land to the west of it?
Describe the relative location of Plymouth to Boston and then to Cape
    Cod.

SOURCES 5 & 6. PHOTOS OF NEW ENGLAND
Describe the physical places shown.
What resources would be available to the settlers?
What hardships might settlers to these areas face?

SUMMARY OF 1–6. DESCRIBE THE GEOGRAPHIC FEATURES OF NEW ENGLAND.

SOURCE 7. DRAWINGS ON THE ECONOMY
Describe the jobs shown here.
What resources would be needed to successfully complete these jobs?

SOURCE 8. DRAWING ON THE ECONOMY
What industry is shown?
What location is needed for this business to operate?
What resource is needed for ships to be built?
What are the main fish that are sold?

SOURCE 9. DRAWING ON THE ECONOMY
What resources are necessary for this business?
How would these mills be powered?

SOURCE 10. TEXT READING
Describe the soil of New England.
Describe the type of farming that was done.

SUMMARY OF 7–10. DESCRIBE THE ECONOMY OF NEW ENGLAND.

SOURCE 11. PICTURE AND DRAWING OF NEW ENGLAND HOMES
What are the houses made of?
How might the shape of the roof be helpful in New England?

Describe the size of the windows. Why would they be designed this way?
Describe the position of the chimney. Why would it be located there? How
is this different from what we saw in the pictures of Southern houses?

SOURCE 12. PICTURE OF THE INSIDE OF A HOUSE
What is the height of the ceilings?
What dominates in this room?
What is it about the geography of this area that might explain your an-
swers to the previous two questions?

SOURCE 13. MAP OF A NEW ENGLAND TOWN
What observations can you make about this New England town?

SOURCE 14. PICTURE OF A NEW ENGLAND TOWN
What observations can you make about this New England town?

SOURCE 15. DRAWING OF BOSTON AND NEW BEDFORD
What observations can you make about why this city and town existed?

SOURCE 16. TEXT READING
Draw a picture of a New England town as described in the text.

SOURCE 17. PICTURE OF A CHURCH IN HINGHAM, MASSACHUSETTS
Look at the roof, windows, walls, and pews. Describe them.
What do you know about the Puritan religion that would explain this ar-
chitecture?

SOURCE 18. MAP OF THE TWELVE LARGEST CITIES
How many of these cities are in New England? Explain why.

*SUMMARY OF 11–18. DESCRIBE A NEW ENGLAND COMMUNITY AND EXPLAIN
WHY IT WAS SET UP AS IT WAS.*

graded them, to ensure that they had successfully completed each phase of
the process necessary if they were to do well at the final stage of major examinations. On the blackboard each day appeared the daily assignments, review sheets due, and upcoming quizzes and exams. Mrs. O justified this emphasis on frequent feedback and assessment as necessary to make explicit to
students exactly what they needed to do to succeed. She also said that she
emphasized "lower-level" concepts in tests because she wanted to reward
careful preparation of reading notes and review sheets, so students would
learn the importance of these steps in attaining mastery of the material.

Mrs. O's classroom agenda reflected her sense of the need to vary activities
and to actively engage students in learning. She displayed a good deal of energy and enthusiasm in all the classes I observed. When working with the
class as a whole, she had a clear agenda she wished to cover, which she

fulfilled by asking students questions and soliciting the answers she wanted. Students often were divided into small groups for part of a class period and given in-class assignments to complete as a group. Mrs. O characterized these to me as inquiry activities. Much of the work in assignment K was carried out in this way. As an in-class activity, each group of four students was provided the relevant set of source materials and asked to work together to answer the questions. The groups I observed were aware that the answers were fairly readily evident in the source materials and did not entail any sustained investigation or deliberation. The answer to a question such as, "What are the houses made of?" for example, could be readily discerned from the photographs provided. Each of the groups I observed divided up the questions among themselves, which was the most efficient way to complete the assignment. The only collaboration involved decisions concerning who would be responsible for which questions.

After five different colonial settlements had been studied, Mrs. O introduced an activity that took several class sessions and was intended as preparation for the final unit exam. Students worked in pairs and chose one of the five settlements to try to "sell back" to Britain. Mrs. O instructed students to promote their colony on the basis of geography, economy, and society (which she defined as the ways people relate). Each pair was required to prepare a poster including a map of the colony and a summary of its attributes and then to use the poster in a presentation to the class. The "sell back" theme suggests that the activity might exercise argument skills, but there was little evidence of this. Students made their presentations and critical comments were solicited, but the presentations were confined almost entirely to describing features of the colony, and no comparisons were made across colonies with respect to any of the specific attributes. (Chapter 6 outlines a later activity involving a debate between loyalists and revolutionaries that has a more explicit argument structure.)

At the class session following completion of the "sell back" project, Mrs. O spent time preparing students for a major unit exam on the colonies. She stressed the links between each of the steps in the process of mastering the material—reading, note-taking, assignments, review sheets, and unit summaries. She stressed the importance of details to support a student's claims. In discussion with me, she noted the importance of understanding in the service of retention—for example, that organizing facts into cause-and-effect relationships (such as the relation between a settlement's geography and economy) aids memory. With students she focused on techniques to use over the weekend to prepare for the test. She stressed, "Don't wait till Sunday night"—the age-old teacher's admonition—but Mrs. O also drew on psychological principles of learning and memory, specifically the superiority of distributed over massed practice. At least three or four times spread over the weekend, she advised, students should spend a twenty-minute period reviewing each colony and each of the characteristics associated with it, making sure they could distinguish between them and not mix them up.

Mrs. O was clearly a dedicated teacher who wanted her students to do well and worked hard toward that end. She had taught four classes a year of seventh-grade American history for many years, with unflagging energy and enthusiasm for her material. She was available every day during a study period after class for students who wanted extra help, and she provided all students detailed feedback on their work. The difference in the sheer amount of information Mrs. O's students and Ms. B's students were exposed to during the same period of time was striking. More difficult to determine was what Mrs. O's (or Ms. B's) students were taking away from the experience. Mrs. O regularly emphasized how essential it was to acquire the academic skills she was teaching because of their importance in students' future school careers. On the other hand, she gave little attention to why the subject matter itself might be important. "What difference does it make what their leisure time activities were?" I overheard one student comment to another, in the rhetorical tone in which no answer is expected. Although it was rare for students to pose such questions to the teacher, I was present when one student asked, "Why do we have to learn the names of all thirteen colonies?" Mrs. O did not hesitate in her reply: "Well, we're going to learn all fifty states by June, so we might as well learn the first thirteen now."

In Chapter 2, I emphasized the importance of the sense students make of what they are doing. Mrs. O's seventh graders seemed convinced by her, as well as by other teachers and their parents, of the importance of learning to do what Mrs. O was asking of them. They seemed to understand that acquiring (or, certainly, retaining) the information itself was less important than developing the skills and discipline necessary to access, organize, and (at least temporarily) retain it. The majority of Mrs. O's students clearly invested a striking amount of effort in this enterprise. They took it on faith from these elders that these skills were essential to their future success. For the most part, they were not being misled in this respect. Getting through Mrs. O's class in seventh grade had the reputation of a "formative experience" that prepared students for the rigors of high school, and that reputation was probably well deserved. Students began to understand what would be expected of them in many of their high-school courses, and they were gearing up for the challenge.

On the other hand, I saw little evidence that students in Mrs. O's class (or in Ms. B's class) were gaining experience in anything we might regard as authentic inquiry learning, despite both teachers' proclaimed intentions. Given its absence in these two classrooms at opposing ends of a continuum, we need to ask whether an agenda of developing inquiry skills in middle-school classrooms is in fact feasible and, if so, how it might be better realized.

Can Inquiry Be Meaningful and Productive?

My purpose in describing the activities I observed in Ms. B's and Mrs. O's classrooms is not to single out their efforts as unusual but instructive cases in which inquiry teaching goes astray, so others might avoid their mistakes. Both teachers made sustained, conscientious efforts to incorporate important intellectual skills into their Social Studies curriculum, indeed to make them its centerpiece. They encountered different problems, but the challenge they faced is shared by all teachers who embrace these goals. Is there any reason to believe that other teachers and students do any better?

What Do Students Do?

Systematic data on students' behavior in inquiry activities in classroom settings are scarce. But the evidence available is consistent with the picture of authentic inquiry as fleeting at best (Krajcik et al., 1998). Krajcik and colleagues observed students engaged in elementary science activities, such as examining the influence of different factors on rate of decomposition. Based on their observations in middle-school classrooms, they characterize students as concentrating more on executing procedures than on what they might learn. Students showed occasional intense interest in an observation, but it was not long-lived enough to sustain cognitive engagement and rarely extended to the scientific implications of the observation. Especially if the data-gathering process was extended, students tended to lose track of the question and the purpose of the data being collected. Students' written reports on their inquiry activities consisted largely of accounts of what they did rather than of what they found out. They did not present an argument in which data were used to justify claims. If both data and conclusions were present, they were likely not to be linked. Finally, students did not relate results to their own knowledge. (Composting and recycling, for example, were familiar everyday issues, yet they did not refer to the results of their study with respect to these problems.)

Krajcik and colleagues conclude that it is necessary to provide more structured support of students' inquiry efforts, in particular by scaffolding the process of question generation, and, throughout the activity, prompting students to identify what their procedures will indicate with respect to the question. In fact, a number of contemporary inquiry curricula—for example, the "learning-by-design" curriculum developed by Kolodner and colleagues (Hmelo, Holton, and Kolodner, 2000) and revised based on classroom observations—have moved in the direction of more highly structured and adult-supported sequences of activities. The danger, of course, as activities become more rigidly prescribed, is that the students' role is reduced to a passive following of adult directions rather than the intended one of directing their own learning. If that happens, students may be left with little sense of why they are doing what they are doing. Yet leaving them on their own to flounder unproductively is hardly a more attractive alternative.

Is Software the Answer?

Sophisticated new educational technology appears to offer teachers just the additional structure needed to support students' inquiry activities. Edelson, Gordin, and Pea (1999), for example, are one of a number of teams of educational technologists who have made a sustained investment in the design of inquiry software for middle- and high-school students. Edelson and colleagues follow an agenda typical of such teams, beginning with construction of an initial program, field testing in classrooms, revision of the program, and return to the field for more testing. They describe four iterations of their program, each successive version based on feedback from teachers who had used the existing version. The content of their software is weather, and the authors are enthusiastic about the vast potential of the technology to provide students with timely, authentic, online data on global weather patterns for several decades, as well as to put into the hands of students "the powerful features of scientists' visualization environments" (p. 403), as the program allows data for multiple variables to be accessed not only numerically but pictorially (in the form of colored maps depicting temperature, with atmospheric pressure as contour overlays and wind speed and direction as vector overlays). The authors express enthusiasm about this database as rich enough to sustain a large variety and number of student investigations centered on a common theme.

Edelson and colleagues recognize the importance of direct observation of students working with the program. In a discussion of next steps, they stress the need for close observation of the program's implementation in classrooms, including assessment of "learning outcomes." Yet their development of the first four versions of the program (over a period of about six years) was guided solely by feedback from teachers who had introduced the software in their classrooms. The major conclusions they draw based on these teacher reports, and consequent modifications they have undertaken, are these:

(a) students need more guidance in formulating questions to put to the data (most students' interest in the first version ended after they had accessed the weather on the date of their birth);

(b) students need to be able to relate the data to their own experience (which led to design of a more structured version, focused on the issue of global warming);

(c) students need to activate their own expectations in advance of seeing the data in order to make sense of it;

(d) students need help in understanding the visualization as a grid of numerical values and utilizing it for the investigation techniques it was designed to support (students used it only to access values in specific locations, rather than for patterns revealed by variations across the display);

(e) it is necessary to precede open-ended investigation with more structured "staging activities," defined as short, structured sets of guiding questions and instructions "designed to build understanding of the relevant investigation techniques and help develop scientific understanding" (p. 422).

The evolution of Edelson and colleagues' inquiry software is typical of design efforts of its type. First, as with most of these efforts, the development of the weather software was not guided by direct observation and analysis of students' behavior when they are engaged with the program. Second, teachers' reports indicate that the capabilities of this program significantly outstripped the ability of the students to engage in the inquiry activities that the technology was designed to support. Third, as teachers reported that students floundered and employed the program unproductively, the authors modified the program to become more structured in the actions that the students were prompted to take and correspondingly restricted the initiative accorded to the student.

If these are the results of inquiry curriculum development efforts, perhaps we should focus attention not on the teaching tool (whether "hands-on" activities or sophisticated computer simulations) but rather on the capabilities that students bring to the tool. Enthusiasm for the capabilities of software has perhaps led software program developers to become absorbed in this potential to an extent that diminishes their attention to the thinking and learning capabilities students bring to the program. What organization do students impose on the activity? What inquiry strategies do they attempt?

And, of greatest importance, in what ways do the skills they display need to develop? Is this last question not worthy of an investment of effort at least equal to that of designing curricula that we presume will develop these skills? It is, in any event, the question of central concern here.

Thesis/Evidence and Cause/Effect as Templates for Elementary Inquiry

If we accept the question just posed as central, a few preliminary answers, at least, are clear. The skills of inquiry are not intuitively given and cannot be assumed to be in place among middle-school students. Nor do they develop on their own, as an outgrowth of young children's "natural" curiosity. The nature and sequence of development of inquiry skills need to be identified in careful detail, and the conditions established that will best support this development. Both Mrs. O and Ms. B., I propose, and all of their counterparts in the range of middle schools from least to most advantaged and enlightened, stand to benefit from a roadmap of what is developing, and what needs to develop, in the way of intellectual skills of inquiry. Such a roadmap is an essential foundation and a continuing guide for effective inquiry activity in classrooms.

A cornerstone of inquiry is the idea of a thesis, or question, and potential evidence that bears on it. Entertaining a thesis that is understood as capable of being disconfirmed by evidence sets the stage for the coordination of theory and evidence that lies at the heart of inquiry. Without this capability, there can be little point to inquiry. At worst, inquiry is reduced to demonstration (of what one already believes to be true), as we see illustrated in Chapter 5, or to the undirected compiling of information toward no particular end, as we observed among both Ms. B's and Mrs. O's students.

Despite their teachers' concerted and varied efforts, students in neither Ms. B's nor Mrs. O's class seemed to have any strong sense of a significant question they might be asking as they engaged in the various inquiry activities their teachers introduced. In both cases, such questions might have lent some purpose and direction to what they were doing. Missing from Ms. B's chart on the research process (see Box 3.1) is any idea of a thesis and evidence bearing on it. The word "compile" (in the sense of *amalgamate*) is used to characterize the key phase of the inquiry process. (Indeed, the chart I observed in another classroom at the struggling school boiled things down even further: It described the research process as composed of four steps: "get information, organize results, plan writing, and write.")

Mrs. O's essay scheme (see Box 3.2) does better in this respect—a "topic sentence" takes the form of a claim and "details" or "proof" the evidence to support it. Yet the emphasis on amassing large quantities of information into this format eclipses any sense of the significance of the question or claim being advanced. Indeed, the cause-and-effect thesis that Mrs. O identified as warranting emphasis as a framework for enhancing under-standing ended up eclipsed by—in fact, relegated to the service of—infor-mation management. She highlighted the students' ability to relate factors as cause and effect (e.g., geography and occupations) primarily as a useful memory aid in their being able to associate characteristics with the correct colonial settlement. Mrs. O was right that organization of factors into cause-and-effect relationships enhances retention, but this emphasis risks neglect of the deeper significance of cause-and-effect relationships, which serve both as evidence for and against claims and as a path to explanation and understanding.

Krajcik and colleagues (1998) advocate the "need to select an overall driv-ing question that can encompass small-scale, student-designed investiga-tions" (p. 343). Although it is more generic than what Krajcik and col-leagues probably have in mind, the "overall driving question" that I would propose as the most promising framework for middle-school students' in-quiry activity is in fact cause and effect. From their earliest years, children construct causal theories as a way of understanding the world around them. A question of cause and effect is immediately accessible and meaningful to children and adults of all ages. Analysis of cause and effect can be appreci-ated as a means to both prediction and control. Questions of cause and ef-fect can be examined in the most elementary form of a single binary (pres-ent or absent) antecedent and an outcome. At the other end of a continuum, inquiry into cause and effect can assume forms as complex as any investigation that takes place in the world of professional science.

What better analytic framework for situating inquiry, then, than cause and effect? The potential content is limitless. Yet disparate content is linked through its common reliance on a generic model. As they engage in inquiry, students are not only constructing mental models of the phenomena they examine but also developing their own more general mental model of how causes and effects operate.

An inquiry framework centered on cause and effect is consistent with cur-riculum standards. The National Science Education Standards under the standard "think critically and logically to make the relationships between evidence and explanations" elaborate: "Specifically, students should be able to review data from a simple experiment, summarize the data, and form a logical argument about the cause-and-effect relationships in the experiment" (National Research Council, 2000, p. 164). I devote most of the next two chapters to exploring what is entailed in developing the cognitive competency that enables a student to do this. A cause-and-effect framework is also sufficiently generic to be compatible with other potential frameworks for inquiry. The learning-by-design inquiry program developed by Kolodner and colleagues (Hmelo, Holton, and Kolodner, 2000), for example, emphasizes engaging students in goal-based activities such as creating balloon-powered and rubber-band-powered propulsion systems. The goal of producing a tangible product can be the "hook" that engages students, but it is far from the endpoint. The objective is to shift students' focus from merely producing an outcome (an "engineering" focus) to analysis of the causal factors responsible for the outcome (a "scientific" focus). Students typically cycle back and forth between the engineering and the scientific focus. It is not a matter of a one-time, once-and-for-all transition from the former to the latter. The pedagogical goal is to ensure that analysis (in this case, cause-and-effect analysis) plays a central enough role in students' endeavors that they have the opportunity to experience and appreciate its powers.

Students must have not only the skills and the opportunity to engage in increasingly complex forms of inquiry. As I argued in Chapter 2, it is equally essential that they develop a firm belief that engaging in inquiry is worthwhile. Such a belief can be grounded only in their own experience. But inquiry experiences have the advantage of revealing their value and power as they are engaged. No further argument for their worth is necessary. Nonetheless, understanding of the nature and value of inquiry itself develops, as do the skills that inquiry requires. As described in Chapter 2, patterns in the development of this epistemological understanding of the nature of knowing have been identified by developmental psychologists, and their findings stand to inform the stated intentions of educators to include understanding *about* inquiry as a curriculum standard (National Research Council, 1996).

The agenda I advocate in this chapter thus requires the joint efforts of educators and researchers in cognitive and developmental psychology. If we can clearly identify what the relevant cognitive skills are and how they develop, we will be in the best position to devise the kinds of exercises that will best promote those skills and will best promote students' understanding of their value. Educators who are informed developmentalists stand to bring the strengths of both traditions to the challenge that meaningful inquiry learning poses.

Learning to learn is an objective that must rank high in just about any educator's agenda. It's hard to think of a more important educational goal. The likelihood of achieving this objective, it would seem, depends at least in part on what we know about the nature of learning.

The topic of learning has been a staple of academic psychology since its early days, and it might be assumed that we already know as much as we need to about how people learn. At this point, however, we know most about what learning is not—namely, the incremental accumulation of facts or associations featured in psychological theories of an earlier era. Nor, to refer to another traditional definition, is it simply a strengthening of behaviors through repetition.

The cognitive revolution of the 1970s transformed the conception of human learning as associations and habits to learning as change in understanding (Schoenfeld, 1999). Psychologists are only beginning to understand the processes involved. In child psychology especially, the study of learning diminished sharply during much of the latter half of the twentieth century and only recently has reemerged in its new identity as the study of changes in understanding. These changes are now often examined via microgenetic methods that focus directly on the process of change itself (Kuhn, 1995; Siegler, 2006). Even more recent is the application of this knowledge to the learning that takes place in schools (Bransford, Brown, and Cocking, 1999).

If we regard learning as change in understanding, what we do know is that such understandings are organized into theory-like entities. Children from an early age construct theories as a means of understanding the world. These theories undergo revision as children interact in the world and encounter evidence bearing on their theories (Gelman and Kalish, 2006). This process of theory-evidence coordination, however, in children's early years does not necessarily take place at a level of conscious awareness or explicit control. Gaining metacognitive control over this process is a major dimension of cognitive development in the years beyond early childhood (Keating, 2004; Kuhn and Franklin, 2006). It is this intentional, controlled theory-evidence coordination, and resulting conceptual change, that is entailed in inquiry learning. In this chapter we examine the skills involved.

Mental Models of Causality

As educators, we should begin by asking what it is that we want students to learn, as this may make a difference. What sorts of understandings might their inquiry learning produce? At the most general level—the only level at which we can hope to answer such a question—we would like students to come to understand the world around them, so as to be able to function effectively in it and achieve their goals. What forms does such knowledge about the world take?

I suggested an answer at the conclusion of Chapter 3 in proposing cause and effect as a framework for students' inquiry. The world consists of complex constellations of multiple forces that act on one another as causes and effects. Even young children construct theories, or mental models, of these causal relations as a means of making sense of both the physical and social phenomena they encounter (Gelman and Kalish, 2006; Keil, 2006). Even before children have names for things, they want to know how they work—what's connected to what?—and these relations are most often construed as causal. Mental models of causal networks do not of course exhaust the kinds of knowledge worth having, but they do constitute a kind of core knowledge that enables us to achieve a satisfactory degree of prediction and control of our environment.

A critical set of cognitive skills, then, are the ones that enable us to extract information from the external world, allowing these mental models to be constructed, elaborated, revised, and updated. Much of this knowledge acquisition, particularly early in life, occurs in an effortless, unconscious manner. To the extent people intentionally engage and control their knowledge acquisition skills, however, their knowledge acquisition capabilities are significantly enhanced. This is what we hope to have happen when we seek to develop students' inquiry learning skills.

The question we begin with, then, is this. What kinds of mental models have people constructed of the causal networks that surround them in their everyday lives? Are these mental models adequate to represent the complexity of the external world? We must address this question before we can go on to examine the task that a learner confronts in inquiry learning—to encounter new evidence and integrate it with existing mental models. As we saw in Chapter 3, the rapidly growing inventory of inquiry software produced for students from elementary school through college age presumes a high level of sophistication in this respect. In the typical inquiry software program, students investigate a set of phenomena that involve multiple causal factors that individually or jointly produce different kinds of outcomes. Their task is to use this new evidence as a basis for revising their existing mental models to become more accurate and comprehensive. It is useful, then, to know something about what these mental models are like.

To examine this question, we can draw on a specific example of a set of causal relations for which many people are likely to have a mental model. The topic is one that the average person has occasion to read and talk about and form ideas about. People also are likely to have personal experiences related to the topic and feel entitled to hold the beliefs they do about it. The topic is why children succeed or fail in school.

People form their causal beliefs based at least in part on an accumulation of everyday observations. Relevant to children's school success, the following are two kinds of observations people are likely to have made:

Children from good homes most often go to good schools and do well.
Children from poor homes quite often go to poor schools and do poorly.

What causal assertions are people likely to make based on an accumulation of such observations? Here are several that it would not be hard to overhear instances of in everyday conversations:

Children need good schools and supportive homes to do well academically.
If children go to good schools, they'll do well even if their home life is poor.
If children get good support at home, they can do well even in a poor school.
It's the children who go to good schools and are supported at home who do really well.

In formal causal language, the first assertion implies that a good home and good schooling are both necessary causes for success. The second assertion implies that good schooling is a sufficient cause of success (and good home life is not necessary). The third assertion implies that a good home is a sufficient cause of success (and good schooling is not necessary). The fourth assertion, however, is ambiguous with respect to the causal claim it makes.

Additive and Interactive Models
The fourth assertion is ambiguous because it does not distinguish between two possible ways in which two causes may jointly affect an outcome. Does

the fourth assertion claim that a good home and a good school each make their own individual contributions to success, contributions that add together when both are present? Or is it saying that children who have good homes and good schools do exceptionally well, better than would be expected from the addition of their individual effects? In the first case, the two causes are referred to as *additive*. In the second case, the two causes are referred to as *interactive*.

Everyday language does not provide an easy way to distinguish these two cases. This fact may make it difficult for people to think about them clearly and appreciate them as different. Compare college students' responses to the two problems in Figure 4.1 (Kuhn, Katz, and Dean, 2004). The wood-stacking problem is a straightforward one that we also administered to sixth graders and found them readily able to solve by simply adding the individual outputs to determine a joint output when individuals worked together. College students produced this same solution.

The pollution problem, however, is less straightforward, and the solution is in fact indeterminate. Two pollutants together may not produce twice the level of pollution as they do individually (there may be a ceiling on the total amount of pollution), or two together may produce more than twice the level of their individual effects (because in combination they are particularly harmful). No sixth graders, however, and only three of thirty-three college students (9 percent) recognized this indeterminacy. One college student predicted a particular form of interactive outcome, and the remaining twenty-nine (88 percent) added the individual effects, producing a solution identical to the one given in the wood-stacking problem. These results are consistent with other findings (Anderson, 1991; Dixon and Tuccillo, 2001) that even young children are able to predict outcomes based on the joint effects of two variables when they are asked explicitly to do so. Yet, the findings just described indicate that even adults tend not to differentiate additive and interactive causes when thinking about multiple factors affecting an outcome.

Too Few Causes or Too Many?

Should we conclude, then, that both adults and children simply add up the effects of multiple causal factors in conceptualizing likely outcomes? And, if so, isn't this a "good enough" approach to get by in most situations? We can bypass the second question, because the answer to the first question is negative. Taking into account and adding up the effects of multiple factors in order to predict an outcome is not what most adults do most of the time. Evidence we turn to shortly shows that many adults, as well as chil-

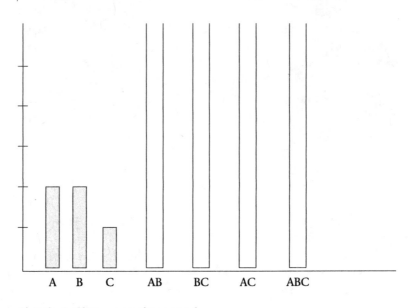

A   B   C   AB   BC   AC   ABC

Al, Bob, & Chris are stacking wood.
The first bar shows how much Al stacks;
the second bar shows how much Bob stacks;
the third bar shows how much Chris stacks.

Fill in the last four bars to show:
How much A&B together stack.
How much B&C together stack.
How much A&C together stack.
How much A,B,&C together stack.

Alt, Bot, & Crel are chemicals that pollute the air and make it dirty.
The first bar shows how much pollution Alt causes.
The second bar shows how much pollution Bot causes.
The third bar shows how much pollution Crel causes.

Fill in the last four bars to show:
How much pollution A&B together cause.
How much pollution B&C together cause.
How much pollution A&C together cause.
How much pollution A,B,&C together cause.

Figure 4.1. Two problems administered to college students and sixth graders.

dren, are unlikely to take into account the multiple factors that potentially affect an outcome. Instead, they make inferences of causality about particular factors, while ignoring the potential effects of others. Moreover, their bases for declaring one factor causal and another noncausal may be faulty. Quite often, they are satisfied to attribute a phenomenon to a single causal factor, among several present, and dismiss the others (a phenomenon known as *discounting*). Moreover, the single factor to which an outcome is attributed is likely to shift over time as successive instances of the outcome are encountered.

To illustrate, consider two more assertions, on the same topic of school failure, that might be overheard in an everyday conversation.

Look how differently children perform in the same classroom, depending on their home background. What the teacher does doesn't really matter.

Even if we assume the truth of the claim made in the first sentence, the form of reasoning is faulty because it ignores the possibility that the factor being discounted (teachers) as not causal may in fact make its own independent contribution to the outcome. Notwithstanding the variety of performance levels in the classroom, it is likely that most students will do better with a good teacher than with a poor one.

Finally, consider this assertion:

The children in this high-performing school are all from good homes. This family influence is important to their success.

In contrast to the previous assertion, in which a potential causal factor is discounted without justification, in this assertion a potential causal factor is inferred to be causal without adequate justification, simply because it co-occurs with the outcome (good family background is present in instances of success).

These causal rules, then, leave the way open for the formation of faulty causal models—models that, moreover, may be resistant to change. A single factor may be regarded as sufficient to account for an outcome, while other, just as worthy candidates are ignored. To achieve this status, it need do no more than occur in the presence of that outcome on at least some occasions. Yet later, it may no longer be seen as having this causal power and the outcome is attributed to a new factor. As the preceding examples illustrate, as well as other more systematic research documents (Kuhn, Amsel, and O'Loughlin, 1988; Kuhn et al., 1995; Schauble, 1990, 1996; Kuhn and Dean, 2004; Kuhn, Katz, and Dean, 2004), these errors are commonplace, rather than exceptions, in the thinking of both children and adults.

Developmental Origins

Seeing these errors of causal reasoning in a developmental framework is useful. Consider the example from five-year-old Danny, whom I asked to explain what makes something alive (Box 4.1). During the course of his explanation, Danny invoked five different attributes as figuring in the definition of being alive: movement, visibility, growth, feeling, and drinking (see summary at end of Box 4.1). Some entities are alive because they possess one of these attributes, while others are not alive because they lack one of them. But, as Danny's explanations clearly reveal, these attributions are entirely uncoordinated. They are not integrated into a consistent, multifactor definition of life. The outcome state (life) is never attributed to more than a single factor. Moreover, a particular factor (e.g., movement) may at one point be alleged as critical to the definition, but later ignored. Hence, sometimes it may be present but the outcome state is not (e.g., the case of wind). In another case, it may be absent and the consequent state nonetheless present (e.g., plants).

Children a few years older than Danny typically have mastered the ability to understand and apply definitions that represent the intersection (an entity must have A *and* B to be defined as X) or addition (an entity must have A *or* B to be defined as X) of two or more characteristics. When this same reasoning structure is transferred to the more complex causal framework, however, we see reemerge conceptual difficulties that parallel those exhibited by Danny. The mental model that appears to govern causal judgments is the one noted earlier: One factor is a sufficient causal explanation of a phenomenon, and that factor need not remain consistent. Factor A causes O in situation *x*, but the cause shifts to factor B in situation *y*. This kind of causal model remains common among adults: "My team won because of skill but the other team's victory was due to luck."

This weak mental model of causality clearly stands in the way of the more comprehensive, powerful, and correct models of additive and interactive multivariable causality that are necessary to accurately represent even simple phenomena in the external world. Most phenomena are affected by multiple causes, and these factors must be regarded as making consistent causal contributions to an outcome in order to represent the way their effects may combine additively or interactively.

What bearing do these conceptual weaknesses have on our topic of inquiry learning? A great deal, it would appear. The typical inquiry learning software we discussed in Chapter 3 presupposes the mature mental model of multivariable causality that has been described in this chapter. In such pro-

Box 4.1 _____

LIFE INTERVIEW WITH DANNY

DK: Are you alive?

Danny: Yes.

DK: What else can you tell me that's alive?

Danny: Mmm. It could be a cat.

DK: A cat. Your cat's alive. Well, what makes something be alive? How do we know that it's alive?

Danny: [pause] I . . . it's moving.

DK: Uh huh. It's moving. Okay. What about wind? When the wind is moving, is it alive?

Danny: No.

DK: Hmm. I thought you said that if something is moving, it's alive. So why isn't the wind alive?

Danny: Because it's not showing.

DK: Not what?

Danny: It's not even showing.

DK: Not showing that it's moving.

Danny: It's not . . . It's not color. It's just like invisible.

DK: Oh. Well, what about water? Sometimes water moves very fast, like in a river.

Danny: That's not alive.

DK: No? Why not?

Danny: Because . . . [shrugs] um, waters have waves and . . . waters . . . water has waves and humans don't.

DK: Oh. So, water is not alive.

Danny: Yes.

DK: And why isn't it alive, even if it moves?

Danny: Because you can splash.

DK: Oh. So that makes it not alive?

Danny: Yeah.

DK: Hmm. Now what about the plants outside? Are they alive?

Danny: Yeah.

DK: Uh huh. Can they move?

Danny: No, but they can . . . but they're still alive.

DK: Well, how do we know? I thought you told me that, in order to be alive, you had to be able to move. So what makes things be alive?

Danny: They have to move, but plants are alive. You know what?

DK: What?

Danny: Plants grow from seeds.

DK: Right.

Danny: So they're alive.

DK: Uh huh. Well, how do we know then, why some things are alive and other things aren't? What are the things you have to do to be alive?

Danny: Move.

DK: You have to move.

Danny: You have to feel the wind.

DK: You have to be able to feel things?

Danny: Mm hmm.

DK: Can plants feel things?

Danny: No.

DK: But are they alive?

Danny: Yes.

DK: So what is it that makes those plants alive?

Danny: Um. They can feel the wind.

DK: Can the plants feel the wind?

Danny: No. They can drink.

DK: OK. All right. And what about a stone? Is a stone alive?

Danny: No! It can't even move.

DK: Oh. So how do we know it's not alive?

Danny: Because it's hard and it can't move.

DK: OK. All right. So would you be able to tell me about anything in the world, whether it's alive or not alive?

Danny: Yeah.

DK: What about one of those germs that you get in your . . . if you have a sore throat and you get a germ in your throat?

Danny: Mmm. You're alive.

DK: Is the germ alive?

Danny: No.

DK: Why not?

Danny: Because it's not even moving.

DK: Oh. That's that thing about moving again. Uh huh. But it's growing, like the plant.

Danny: Yeah.

DK: 'Cause you know, sometimes germs grow bigger. So could it be alive because it's growing?

Danny: It couldn't. No, it's not.

DK: It just can't be alive?

Danny: No, it can't.

DK: Is it like a stone?

Danny: Yeah.

DK: Uh huh. It doesn't have any of the things that make it alive?

Danny: Yeah.

Summary of Danny's definition of life

A cat is alive because it moves.	A stone is not alive because it doesn't move.
Plants are alive because they grow.	A germ is not alive because it doesn't move.
Plants are alive because they feel the wind.	The wind is not alive because it is invisible.
Plants are alive because they drink.	Water is not alive because it can be moved by human agents.

grams, as in everyday life, multiple potential causal influences on a phenomenon coexist and it is necessary to analyze the available evidence in order to conceptualize how these factors, individually and jointly, influence outcomes. If students of the ages at which inquiry learning is being introduced lack a mature mental model of causality, one adequate to the task of representing how a set of multiple factors influence an outcome, what happens when they are asked to bring new evidence to bear on such a model—the task posed by inquiry learning?

Coordinating Mental Models with New Evidence

Mental models ordinarily remain hidden from view. One way to make them more observable is to present some new evidence and ask an individual to interpret it. This approach may reveal either or both of two kinds of weaknesses. One, which we have already considered, is a mental model that is not adequate to represent the relations involved. The other is weak or faulty inference strategies for interpreting new evidence and reconciling it with this model. Coordinating new evidence with existing mental models of a domain is exactly what students are asked to do in inquiry learning. How, then, do they approach this task?

Interpreting Selected Evidence

Consider the problem presented in Box 4.2. The causal relations that can be inferred from the data in the box are summarized in Figure 4.2. Although only one factor (teacher aide) can be examined and shown to have a causal effect in isolation, available comparisons make it possible to infer a causal

Box 4.2
___

WHICH FACTORS AFFECT READING PERFORMANCE?

A school district is experimenting with new methods of improving beginning reading instruction. In different classrooms across the district, they are instituting a new reading curriculum, teacher aides, and reduced class size. Here are some preliminary results.

Type of classroom	Average reading performance
Regular	Poor
New curriculum & teacher aide	Greatly improved
New curriculum & reduced class size	Improved
Teacher aide & reduced class size	Improved
New curriculum, teacher aide, & reduced class size	Greatly improved
Teacher aide	Improved

- What conclusions do you draw from these findings? Justify your answers by referring to the data.
- Is the new curriculum beneficial? How do you know?
- Is the teacher aide beneficial? How do you know?
- Is the reduced class size beneficial? How do you know?

effect of curriculum or an absence of causal effect of class size by making one of the comparisons shown in Figure 4.2.

The urban community college students to whom we presented the problem (Kuhn et al., 2004) responded in a way consistent with the causal underattribution (discounting) and, especially, overattribution illustrated earlier. They very rarely judged class size as having no causal effect. Instead, the overattribution illustrated earlier is the dominant response: Whatever factors are present in the context of an outcome contribute to that outcome. Hence a typical response regarding the new curriculum was:

Yes it is [beneficial], because all the cases where a new curriculum has been applied the class has improved.

The reasoning was similar with respect to class size, despite its actual noncausal status:

Class size is also beneficial because, according to the data, improvement was evident.

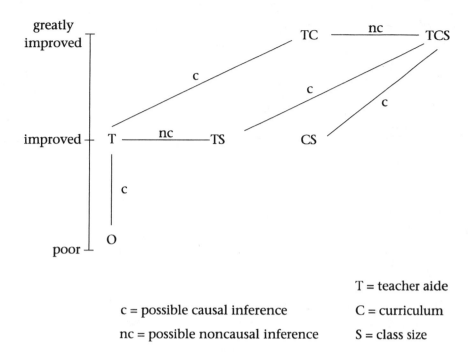

Figure 4.2. Possible inferences in reading performance problem (Box 4.2).

Or,

Yes, one case shows [class size] greatly improved performance.

Underattribution of causality was not absent among these students, but the most common basis for it was to ignore the evidence entirely and resort to their own beliefs for justification. For example:

A teacher aide is not beneficial because each teacher has their own method of teaching, so a teacher aide can create confusion.

Even when the data did support exclusion of a factor as having causal power, this ignoring of the data (despite explicit instruction to evaluate it) and exclusive reliance on prior beliefs were common. For example:

Yes, reduced class size makes a difference because the numbers of children are small so they can learn better and faster.

This last response has particularly important implications. Inquiry learning requires that students encounter new information and interpret it. If warranted, they are able to revise their existing understandings accordingly. Alternatively, it is entirely reasonable that they will reject the new information they have examined because they regard it as flawed or irrelevant. The students responding to the problem in Box 4.2 were free to indicate that the data supported a certain conclusion but that they rejected this conclusion because of disbelief in the data or because of the strength of other knowledge they had that supported a different conclusion.

What is important, then, is not whether the students decided to revise their existing beliefs, based on the new information, but rather the process leading to this decision. To judge what to make of this information, students had to evaluate it in its own right—to interpret exactly what it did or did not imply. The students had to then connect it to what they already knew or understood. To do this, students, first and foremost, had to be aware of what they thought and knew. They had to be able to think about their own thinking, as an object of cognition. Only then could they accomplish the integration of what they already knew and what they were discovering from a new source. This is what we mean by the consciously controlled coordination of theory and evidence, and this is what we expect to happen during inquiry learning.

What we often find, instead, is a lack of firm differentiation between conclusions based on existing understandings and conclusions based on new evidence. At the critical metacognitive level—the level of thinking about thinking—students are not clearly aware of whether a claim they are making is based on existing beliefs or new information. Hence they are not in control of the process of theory-evidence coordination.

Consider as an example this response from one community college student to the problem in Box 4.2. Regarding the new curriculum, she first of all claimed:

> Yes it is [beneficial] because according to the data those with the new curriculum were doing better.

Her reasoning reflects the same flaw identified earlier (overattribution of causality to any factor associated with the outcome), but she was endeavoring to interpret the evidence before her. Next she considered the teacher aide and claimed:

> Yes because with it I guess the teacher could really get through to the students. Thus, the improvement.

Here she allowed her own sense of why this causal effect was plausible to enter in, as an explanation for the data, to which she does refer. By the time she got to a consideration of the final factor, however, she had abandoned any reference to the evidence, allowing it to be eclipsed entirely by her own ideas:

> Yes [class size matters], because it helps the teacher to pay special attention to each student and draw out those who need the most attention and help them.

By this point, the student appears to have lost any metacognitive awareness of whether it was her own knowledge or the newly presented evidence that motivated her claims.

Selecting Evidence for Interpretation

In another kind of task, which I turn to more fully in Chapter 5, we asked community college adults, as well as children, to select their own observations to examine from a multivariable database and to draw inferences about how the variables were related (Kuhn et al., 1995)—a paradigm that brings us closer to inquiry learning. One of the databases, for example, consists of children's popularity ratings of TV programs that vary on five different features. Commonly, adults as well as children change their judgments multiple times during the course of their investigations, alleging, for example, that one TV program is popular because it has music but later attributing the popularity of another program to a different feature—such as humor—and indicating that in that case the presence or absence of music was irrelevant. The faulty inference rules that are applied, usually in the service of protecting prior beliefs, are illustrated by the reasoning portrayed by Geoff in Box 4.3 (from Kuhn et al., 1995).

Could it be that Geoff's inconsistent and faulty causal attribution was due entirely to the conflict he experienced between what he expected to be true and what the data suggested? In other research, children and adults have been asked to reason in domains in which they are less likely to hold strong prior theories. Similar characteristics are nonetheless evident. Keselman (2003) asked sixth graders to investigate and make inferences regarding the causal role of five variables that had been identified within a domain (variables affecting earthquake risk); the students were also asked to make outcome predictions for two new cases representing unique combinations of levels of variables within the domain. After each prediction, a student was asked, "Why did you predict this level of risk?" The variables that a student mentioned were taken as *implicit* judgments of the variable's causality. The

Box 4.3

EXAMPLE OF ONE STUDENT'S PERFORMANCE ON THE TV PROBLEM

The first program Geoff (a pseudonym) selected to examine had commercials but no music or humor, was two hours long, and on Tuesday, with a popularity rating of fair. Geoff interpreted this outcome as confirming his earlier expressed theories:

> You see, this shows you that the factors I was saying about, that you have to be funny to make it good or excellent, and the day doesn't really matter, and it's too long.

The second instance Geoff chose added humor and music and changed the length to a half hour and the day to Wednesday, with an outcome of excellent. Now Geoff concludes, based on the two instances:

> It does make a difference when you put music and have commercials and the length of time and the humor. Basically the day is the only thing that doesn't really matter.

Geoff thus utilized these two pieces of evidence as an opportunity to confirm his initial theories. Three factors that covaried with outcome (music, humor, and length) he interpreted as causal. He also included commercials as causal even though it did not vary, but excluded day of week, which did vary, as noncausal. He selects data for observation that he believes will "illustrate" the correctness of these theories. To the extent the outcome data pose interpretive problems, he draws on a variable set of inference rules, applying to each variable those rules that are most protective of his theories. Presence or absence of commercials, for example, is implicated as causal based on its presence in just one successful outcome. When possible, however, in the case of the three other variables also believed causal, Geoff applies the more stringent covariation rule as the basis for inferring causality. As Geoff's reasoning illustrates, the explanatory burden shifts from one variable to another in a way that allows theories to be maintained.

variables students named earlier as causal (in announcing their postinvestigation conclusions) were taken as *explicit* causal judgments.

Consistency between explicit and implicit causal judgments was low. Over half of the students justified one or both of their predictions by implicating a variable they had earlier explicitly concluded to be noncausal. More than 80 percent failed to implicate as contributing to the outcome one or more variables they had previously explicitly claimed to be causal. Overall, fewer features were implicated as contributory in the implicit attributions than were explicitly stated to be causal. Students showed low consistency not only between explicit and implicit causal theories but also in the consistency of causal attribution across the predictions. Almost three quarters of the students failed to implicate the same variable(s)as having causal power across both prediction instances. Finally, roughly half of the students justified each of their predictions by appealing to the effect of only a single variable.

Findings were not that different among adults (Kuhn and Dean, 2004), in this case, members of a community choral group and hence representative of a broad cross-section of the population. Over half showed inconsistency in causal attribution in the course of their successive interpretations of accumulating evidence, either at least once initially judging a variable as noncausal and later judging it to be causal, initially judging a variable as causal and later judging it noncausal, or showing both inconsistencies. Similarly, over half showed inconsistency between implicit and explicit causal judgments. Almost half were inconsistent in causal attributions across three prediction questions. Like the sixth graders, these adults failed to implicate as causal in their implicit attributions as many variables as they needed to in order to yield correct predictions. Over a quarter appealed to the effect of only a single (usually shifting) variable in their prediction judgments, and over half appealed to the effect of only two of the four variables.

Again, then, we can identify an inadequate mental model of multivariable causality as a constraint on both children's and adults' ability to interpret evidence involving effects of multiple variables on an outcome. Also constraining their reasoning are faulty inference rules that allow factors to be judged causal due simply to their association with the outcome (overattribution) and to be judged noncausal because one or more other factors are assumed responsible for the outcome (underattribution, or discounting).

The most fundamental constraint, however, and the one that most directly and seriously undermines inquiry learning, is lack of firm differentiation between inferences deriving from existing beliefs and inferences deriving from the evaluation of new evidence. Why is this so? If students are not clear whether their claim is based on their existing beliefs or on the new information they have examined—and in the latter case, if they are not clear about what that information is—they are not in control of the process of theory-evidence coordination in their own thinking. Inquiry learning, for such students, is at best a limited enterprise. They may learn a little about their topic, but they will not be learning how to learn.

Developmental Origins

Again it is useful to see these weaknesses in a developmental framework. In a study of four- to six-year-olds (Kuhn and Pearsall, 2000), we hypothesized that children would fail to distinguish between theoretical explanations and evidence as a basis for their simple knowledge claims, in a parallel way to the confusion between theory and evidence as justifications for more complex causal inferences that we had observed in older children and adults (Kuhn, 1989; Kuhn et al., 1988, 1995). Children were shown a sequence of pictures in which, for example, two runners compete in a race. A cue suggests a theoretical explanation concerning why one will win—for example, one has fancy running shoes and the other does not. The final picture in the sequence provides evidence of the outcome: One of the runners holds a trophy and exhibits a wide grin. When children are asked to indicate the outcome and to justify this knowledge, four-year-olds show a fragile distinction between the two kinds of justification, "how do you know?" and "why is it so?"—in other words, the evidence for their claim (the outcome cue in this case) versus their explanation as to why it is plausible (the theory-generating cue). Rather, the two merge into a single representation of what happened, and the child tends to choose as evidence of what happened the cue having greater explanatory value as to why it happened. Thus, in the race example, young children often answered the "how do you know [he won]?" question not with evidence ("he's holding the trophy") but with a theory of why this state of affairs makes sense ("because he has fast sneakers").

Similarly, in another set of pictures in which a boy is shown first climbing a tree and then down on the ground holding his knee, the "how do you know [that he fell]?" question was often answered, "Because he wasn't holding on carefully." These confusions between theory and evidence diminish sharply among six-year-olds, who still make mistakes but who usually distinguish the evidence for their event claim from a theoretical explanation that makes the claim plausible. Findings by other investigators support this characterization of preschool children as having weak metacognitive control of their own knowing, failing to differentiate different sources of their own knowledge claims (Gopnik and Graf, 1988; Robinson, 2000) and claiming that they had "always known" a piece of information they had just been given (Taylor, Esbensen, and Bennett, 1994).

This meta-level management and control of knowing develops only gradually. From its origins in these early years, sufficient awareness needs to develop to enable an individual to answer the critical question, "How do I know?" in any context. Cognitive psychologists have studied people's reliance on evidence versus explanation in justifying their claims and found explanation the clear winner. Awareness of a plausible mechanism that could explain a link between cause and effect is a more powerful factor motivating a causal inference than is evidence supporting the existence of a causal relationship (Ahn et al., 1995; Ahn and Bailenson, 1996; Brem and Rips, 2000; Kuhn, 2001). Similar to the young children in the research just described, in more complex contexts of causal inference, even adults are likely to conclude that their claim that A is the underlying cause of B is right because it makes sense to them that it should be so—it seems right.

The danger of this kind of reasoning, of course, is that all thought stops there. The epistemological weaknesses of claims resting on explanation rather than evidence are well known: They lead to overconfidence, they inhibit examination of alternatives, and, most seriously, they may be false. In developing skills of inquiry in students, it is just these weaknesses in thinking that we would like to see overcome.

What Needs to Develop?

Why have we spent so much time in this chapter examining the reasoning of adults in a book about educating children and adolescents? If, as I have claimed, adults often do not have command of the cognitive skills that underlie inquiry, we cannot presume they are in place in children or adolescents. Much emphasis in the current enthusiasm for inquiry learning as the centerpiece of a contemporary curriculum has been on making rich sources of information available, especially via the Internet, letting students conceive their own questions and affording them the freedom to pursue those questions. Too little attention has been paid to identifying the intellectual skills that students need to develop if they are to make use of modern technology not as an end in itself but as a resource in the service of inquiry.

In this chapter we have examined fundamental cognitive skills that effective inquiry learning presupposes, skills that do not appear to be in the repertory of the typical middle-school student. The most fundamental is the recognition that there is something to find out—in other words, the understanding that the data being examined can be analyzed and interpreted in a manner that will bear on the claims under consideration. The differing epistemological status of the two—claim and evidence—must be recognized. This distinction between theory (what makes sense to me) and evidence, as sources of knowing, is essential to maintain, or it becomes impossible to construct relations between them.

We want students to overcome the temptation to cling to their existing explanations of the way things are as "good enough" ways of knowing the world and to understand and therefore value inquiry as a path to purposefully enriching their existing understandings. As well as having the conviction that there is something to find out, they must see "finding out" as worth the effort it entails. If they do not, despite educators' best intentions, inquiry activities run the risk of being reduced to undirected search for something that might turn out to be interesting or, alternatively, simply demonstration of what is already taken to be true. In the latter case, the inquiry context becomes an opportunity to "illustrate" what the student already conceives of as the way things are, rather than a context of discovery and analysis.

Once the relevance of evidence is established, students must come to see *analysis* of it—the identification of patterns and relationships—and the coordination of what is observed with existing understandings, as a path to enhanced understanding. They must become practiced in the purposeful and consciously controlled coordination of theory and evidence. If a student uses inquiry activities only to create an effect—to make something happen—rather than in the service of analysis, inquiry will yield no knowledge dividends. Even with analysis adopted as a goal, the student still confronts the demanding task of developing valid inference strategies for interpreting the multiple causes and effects that most phenomena entail and understanding how they intersect additively or interactively in consistent, and therefore predictable, ways.

In the next chapter, I describe obstacles that students encounter in navigating this developmental course in a context of self-directed inquiry, one in which they are able to select instances for examination and thereby design their own investigations. In some cases, we will see, given ample opportunity to engage in simple inquiry activity, students develop these skills without assistance. In other cases, students' inquiry efforts suggest that they are at a standstill. Hence, we examine the kinds of cognitive scaffolding that might be provided if our goal is one of ensuring that meaningful inquiry activity lies within the grasp of every student.

This chapter turns to observations of middle-school students in the process of developing the skills introduced in Chapter 4. The context for this development is a database of instances, usually accessed via computer. Working individually or collaboratively, students choose cases to examine with the goal of drawing conclusions regarding how the depicted factors relate to one another. The goals of the activity are thus typical of many inquiry curriculum units, although in this case students have the freedom, not always afforded in inquiry curricula, to direct their own investigations.

The Inquiry Environment

The structure underlying the database students investigate consists of a network of causal relations. Observations of the levels of skill that middle-school students typically bring to this activity led us to reduce the initial level of complexity of this structure to a minimum. The five features introduced as potential causal agents in producing an outcome are dichotomous (they can assume one of only two levels). Some of the features in fact have no effect and others have simple additive effects on this outcome. If students conduct effective investigations, they are able to identify the causal and noncausal factors and hence to predict outcomes of specific feature constellations, enabling them to appreciate the value of their analytic efforts.

The goal of the inquiry experience is to foster the development of inquiry skills, not to teach science (or other) content. It does not follow that the activity involves no meaningful content. Students bring a rich array of existing knowledge to their contemplation of the data that are made available to them to examine. Although the structure of the causal relations reflected in these data is simple, students' ideas about them are not. Omitting nonessential content from the presented data, we have found, enables both student

79

and observer to focus on the processes by which one identifies, makes use of, and integrates new information.

An example of such an inquiry environment is the earthquake problem, introduced in Figure 5.1, in which students seek to identify the factors affecting earthquake risk. No direct instruction is provided, but students are asked probing questions to promote reflection such as, "What do you want to find out about?" and "What do these results show?"

Students engage in the activity not just once but on multiple occasions, typically once or twice a week over a period of months. Microgenetic analysis (Kuhn, 1995; Siegler, 2006) documents the changes that occur during this period of repeated engagement. In this case it is possible to track dual forms of change, first in a student's increasing understanding of the causal structure underlying the database of observations and, second, in advances in the investigative and inference strategies a student uses to generate this knowledge (Kuhn, Schauble, and Garcia-Mila, 1992; Kuhn et al., 1995; Schauble, 1990, 1996; Kuhn and Pearsall, 1998; Kuhn et al., 2000; Keselman, 2003). This chapter examines how students' inquiry skills advance as they engage in these inquiry activities over an extended period.

We have now explored a number of different content domains in which to situate the activity, in addition to the earthquake domain illustrated here. Interestingly, students of middle-school age find most appealing those topics having to do with everyday phenomena—for example, the features of TV shows that affect their popularity among children. They find it easy and enjoyable to think about such topics, although, we have found, they do not find it as easy to think well about them as they do about more "scientific" topics in natural science domains, to which they typically bring less well-formed ideas. Teachers, in contrast, are much more comfortable, we have found, with more traditional science topics (and hence more willing to have their students spend time engaged with them), and this fact has driven our more frequent use of mainstream science content—for example, earthquakes and avalanches—as well as less typical content like TV shows and music clubs.

Phases of Inquiry Activity

This section examines three broad phases of the inquiry process—inquiry, analysis, and inference—and within each identifies the specific task demands it poses. Also identified are the kinds of strategies, from less to more effective, that we have observed students to use in engaging these task demands.

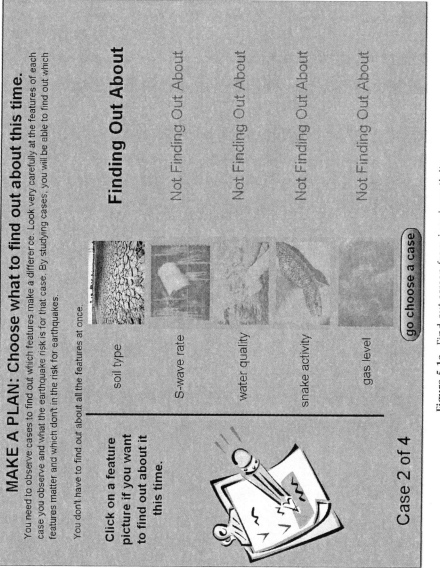

Figure 5.1a. Find-out screen from inquiry activity.

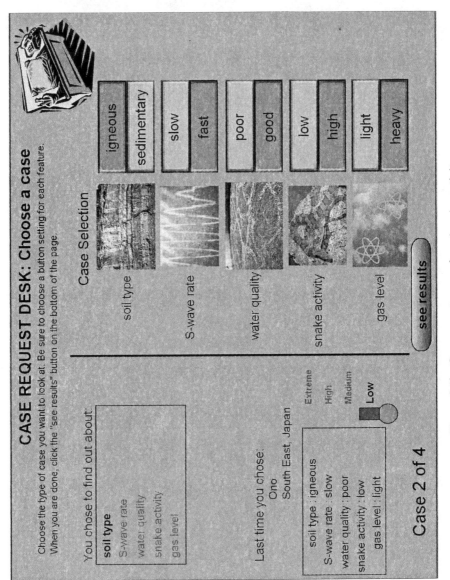

Figure 5.1b. Case-request screen from inquiry activity.

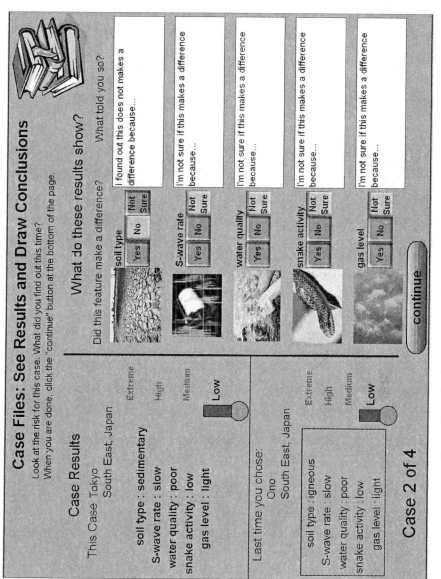

Figure 5.1c. Analysis-and-inference screen from inquiry activity.

Inquiry

As the foundation of authentic inquiry, the initial inquiry phase is crucial. It is the phase in which the student identifies (or not) a purpose of the activity. As Chapter 4 concludes, for inquiry to be meaningful, students must believe there is something to find out, distinguishable from what they already know. And they must see themselves as engaging in inquiry activity for the purpose of finding it out and for the purpose of reconciling what they find out with what they already know.

On the grounds that there is no clear dividing line between informal and formal theories, we refer here to a student's mental representation of the way things are, no matter how simple, implicit, or fragmentary, as a theory, rather than reserve the latter term for theories meeting various formal criteria (Brewer and Samarapungavan, 1991). During inquiry activity, such theories, or components of them, provide the claims that a student may seek to examine, and possibly revise, in the light of evidence.

Young children's theory revision occurs implicitly and effortlessly, most often without conscious awareness or intent (see Chapter 4). Young children think *with* their theories, rather than about them. The intention to seek knowledge transforms implicit theory revision into intentional inquiry, or what may also be called scientific thinking (Kuhn, 2002). Theory revision becomes something I *do*, rather than something that happens to me outside of conscious awareness. The process of theory-evidence coordination becomes explicit and intentional.

When discrepancy between theory and evidence appears, relations between the two need to be constructed. This coordination requires encoding and representation of the evidence as an entity distinct from the theory, which is itself explicitly represented as an object of cognition. Only then can relations between the two be constructed. The outcome of the process, note, remains open. It is not necessary that the theory be revised in light of the evidence, nor certainly that theory be ignored in favor of evidence, which is a misunderstanding of what is meant by theory-evidence coordination. The evidence may be rejected as flawed or insufficient to warrant a revision of the theory. The criterion is only that the evidence be represented in its own right and its implications for the theory examined.

The inquiry phase is depicted in Figure 5.2. The task objectives appear at the left. The ovals at top center represent the student's attempt to engage the objectives and his or her meta-level monitoring of these efforts. At the right appear the strategies that have been observed on the part of students as they undertake this inquiry. Strategies are ordered from the least effective

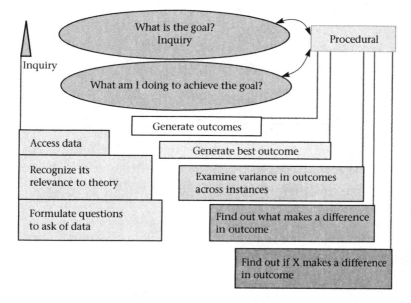

Figure 5.2. The inquiry phase.

at the top (generate outcomes) and proceed sequentially to the increasingly more effective.

To illustrate some of these strategies, I begin with an excerpt of the early investigations of Brad, a sixth grader at the best-practice school who will in another year be in Mrs. O's Social Studies class. Brad is investigating the earthquake database. Two of the five features—type of soil (igneous or sedimentary) and speed of S waves (slow or fast)—have no effect on risk, while the other three—water quality (good or poor), radon gas levels (light or heavy), and snake activity (high or low)—have simple additive effects on outcome.

While selecting the second instance he wanted to examine from the database, Brad commented:

Last time, the [sedimentary] rock was like white. This one [igneous] is sort of like not. It looks like it's going to just blow up any second. This [sedimentary] one looks like it's okay. (So which one do you want to choose to investigate?) Sedimentary. (Why?) Because last time I chose sedimentary as well and it seemed to work out pretty good. The igneous looks like it's about to explode any second.

Brad thus showed a strategy more advanced than that of some of his peers, who wanted to "just try different things and see what happens." He sought to produce a "good" or "best" outcome. Yet his efforts at this point did not reflect an appreciation of the goals of inquiry. He did not appear to understand the purpose of examining instances to be that of obtaining information that would allow him to proceed to the next phases of the inquiry process, analysis and inference. He had not formulated a question to put to the data he generated.

Brad's classmate Tom exhibited a more advanced level of investigation in which he set out to identify effects of individual features. Two characteristics, however, limited the effectiveness of Tom's investigations. First, he believed he could find out the effects of all features at one time and hence did not focus his inquiry on any particular feature. Second, he did not mentally represent the evidence he generated in a form that was distinct from his theories.

In response to the first instance he chose to examine, Tom noted the outcome of highest risk level. Contrary to Brad, Tom did not regard producing a good (low-risk) outcome as the goal, and commented:

> I'm feeling really good about this. (Why?) Like I said before on everything. The water quality being poor. Obviously the earthquake would contaminate the water in some way. The S-waves would go fast because logically thinking even big earthquakes happen pretty quickly. Gas, I figured it'd be kind of hard to breathe in an earthquake. Like I said before about the snakes, in the 1986 earthquake, dogs started howling before it happened.

Tom could, of course, draw no conclusions from this single instance of evidence, but an even more fundamental problem was his failure to clearly represent the evidence as such. In fact, Tom saw his empirical observation not so much as a test of, or even evidence bearing on, his theories as it was simply an "illustration" of the theories he had voiced prior to beginning his investigations. Tom was "feeling good" because his theories had, from his perspective, withstood the test of empirical confirmation. In reality, of course, they had not been tested at all.

Analysis

To negotiate the analysis phase, depicted in Figure 5.3, Tom needed to be able to examine and interpret the evidence he had generated with respect to its bearing on a thesis he had identified. Tom's efforts highlight how limited fulfillment of the objectives of the initial inquiry phase constrain progress in the analysis phase. In the second instance he chose to examine (in which

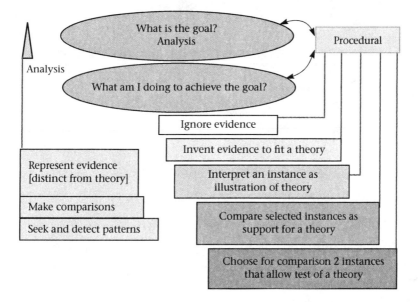

Figure 5.3. The analysis phase.

the levels of three of the five features were changed), Tom observed the risk fall to medium-high and commented:

Type of soil makes no difference. No actually it makes a difference. Snake activity makes a difference. And water quality . . . hmm, yeah it brought it down. That was probably half the reason that lowered [the risk] down, with the soil and the S-wave. Soil made a difference I think because it lowered it down because . . . well, it [sedimentary] seemed less threatening, so I figured it lowered it down. Snake activity, like I said before, animals act up before disasters happen.

Note the overriding role that theory played in Tom's implicating the type of soil as bearing some responsibility for the reduced risk. Snake activity, note also, Tom implicated as causal even though it remained at an unchanged (high) level in both of the instances he had observed by that point. Tom was queried about this feature:

(Suppose someone disagreed and said that snake activity makes no difference. What would you tell them? Could you tell them that you found out here that it did make a difference?) Well, if you did it low, probably everything's normal because the snakes wouldn't be acting up in some odd way.

Thus, Tom's claim rested on hypothetical evidence (regarding low snake activity) that he had not in fact obtained. A similar exchange occurred regarding gas level, which also had remained at the same (heavy) level across the two instances; and this time, Tom did not even make reference to evidence:

> The gas makes a difference because the heavier it is, the harder it would be to breathe. (Suppose someone disagreed and said that gas level makes no difference. How could you show them that you're right? Did you see anything here that shows you that it does make a difference?) Well, I think it makes a difference because . . . Let me summarize this up. When it's heavy there are more things in the air to clog up your lungs.

Finally, based on the two available instances, Tom again implicated water quality, which has covaried with outcome, as causal. He changed his mind about S-wave rates, however, which also covary with outcome, eventually claiming this feature to be noncausal:

> Water quality makes a big difference. If it's good it wouldn't be contaminated by an earthquake, which also brought [risk] down. And the S-waves, they're going slowly, always moving. So they don't really make a difference.

These excerpts from Tom's investigative activity show that when data are not represented in their own right, distinct from theory, the potential for analysis is limited. Tom's references to evidence he had generated served at most to illustrate the theories he had brought to the situation. The evidence was not capable of disconfirming a theory, nor even of standing apart from the theory and bearing on it. Note also how important it was to Tom to make theoretical sense of the instances he was observing. Never did he acknowledge an association (between feature level and outcome) without providing a theoretical explanation of it. Thus, even though with continued engagement, students like Tom are likely to develop increasing sensitivity to evidence, accurate reading of the data remains constrained by the need to make theoretical sense of what is being observed. For Tom, the data never stood on their own, representing a state of affairs that might depart from the way he believed things to be.

Inference

The inference phase, depicted in Figure 5.4, is the culmination of inquiry. The investigator must come to terms with what has been accomplished: What can I claim and how do I know? In his initial comments, following the first instance he generated, Tom was quite ready to interpret

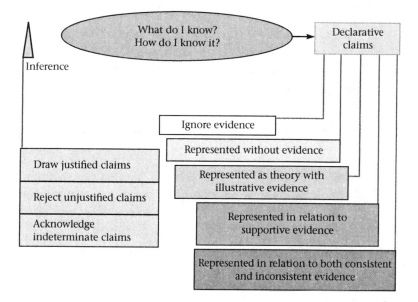

Figure 5.4. The inference phase.

multiple features as causally implicated in an outcome, based on a single co-occurrence of one level of the feature and an outcome. He did not see controlled comparison (in which all features except the one of interest are held constant), or even any comparison across instances, as essential to allow valid inference. Nor, when he generated a second instance that varied from the first with respect to three features, did he recognize the comparison of the two instances as incapable of demonstrating the operation of any particular causal factor.

Another classmate at the best-practice school, Mark, did better than Tom in representing data separately from his theories and drawing on these data as a basis for his inferences. In other respects, however, his approach was like Tom's. Mark implicated features as causal based on a single co-occurrence of variable level and outcome. In choosing an instance for observation, he intended "to try to find out about everything"; and in choosing a second instance, he decided to "do the opposite of each one." Mark saw the risk level drop (from instance 1 to 2) from medium-high to low risk. In interpreting the second outcome, he implicated four of the five varying features as causal (with the justification that they covaried with outcome) and yet dismissed the fifth (for which the evidence was identical) on the basis of his belief that this feature made no difference.

Both Mark's and Tom's inferences were consistent with what I have called a co-occurrence mental model of causality. Both boys falsely included as causal a feature that either co-occurred with outcome in a single instance or covaried with outcome over two instances. In so doing, both made serious inferential errors in overattributing causality to factors that had not in fact been established as playing a causal role. The underattribution of causality described in Chapter 4 also appears. In choosing a third instance for examination, Mark changed some features and left others the same and observed a low-risk outcome. Following causal inferences for several features, Mark made two noncausal inferences for features that showed no variation over the two instances. Water quality, Mark concluded, made no difference because:

> before [instance 1] it was good and had medium-high risk. This time it's good and has low risk. (What does that tell you?) It probably doesn't matter.

The implication was that another feature had produced the variation, illustrating that feature's causal power in affecting the outcome, and the feature in question could therefore be discounted. Mark's inference regarding snake activity was identical in form.

Both the overattribution and underattribution errors were consistent with the co-occurrence model of causality (the co-occurrence of a level of one variable and an outcome is sufficient to explain that outcome). The potential causal influence of a second variable, therefore, need not be treated as additive. Instead, the second variable can be momentarily ignored but then may be invoked as a different explanation for a later outcome, or the second variable can be discounted because the first variable explains the outcome. Thus, the co-occurrence mental model treats causal influences as neither consistent nor additive, the two attributes Chapter 4 identified as essential to a mature mental model of multivariable causality.

Taking into account all causal effects that are operating is of course the only way to achieve the goals of correct representation of a causal system and accurate prediction of outcomes. Doing so requires a mental model of causality in which multiple causes operate additively and consistently. (Interactive effects require a still more advanced level of understanding.)

The immature mental model of causality reflected in Tom's and Mark's inquiry activity, then, limits adoption of either the goals or strategies that make for effective inquiry. Unsurprisingly, neither Mark's nor Tom's investigations led to judgments of any greater-than-chance correctness. Mark, for example, concluded (after examining four instances) that all features except water quality were causal. He was wrong about three of the five features.

Also at an immature level in students like Tom and Mark is metacognitive awareness of the success of their inquiry activities. When asked how sure he was that he had found out which features did and did not make a difference, on a 1 to 10 scale, Mark rated his certainty as 9.

Developing Effective Inquiry Skills

In studies of students working on the earthquake and other comparable problems, my colleagues and I have found an association between the intention to identify the effect of an individual feature and the use of controlled comparison as an investigative strategy (Kuhn et al., 2000). This may be so because both are supported by a mature additive mental model of causality. In the absence of this model, the goal is unlikely to be identification of the effect of each of the individual features, to determine their cumulative effects (because one feature alone is usually regarded as sufficient to explain the effect). Moreover, neither attribute of a controlled comparison strategy is likely to be recognized as important. The "comparison" attribute is not compelling, given its purpose is to assess the effect of individual variables. The "controlled" attribute is even less compelling, because it is the individual effects of other variables that need to be controlled. An immature mental model of causality, then, limits adoption of either the goals or strategies that make for effective inquiry.

How does development of these goals and strategies occur? Our microgenetic studies indicate that, in many (although not all) cases, the opportunity to engage frequently in inquiry activity is sufficient to foster change. These studies, moreover, have allowed us to observe something about the manner in which this development occurs. The case study of Beth, a student at a school similar to the best-practice school, is a good illustration. Her progress was striking (although not atypical), especially because she was only a fourth grader and thus several years younger than Brad, Tom, and Mark. She began at a developmental level not unlike that of the three boys and yet, in the course of several months of focused inquiry activity, she progressed to a moderately skilled level of inquiry.

Beth worked simultaneously in two different inquiry domains, devoting one weekly session to each. One was a computerized environment in which the objective was to determine the effects of the various features of racecars on their speed across a simulated track. The other involved actual model boats that traveled down a five-foot-long water canal via a weight-and-pulley apparatus. The objective similarly was to determine the effects of various features on the boats' speed. (See Kuhn et al., 1992, for further details.)

Boat Domain

We examine Beth's progress here primarily in the context of her boat investigations, but later I describe the indications of parallel progress in her investigation of the cars. The boat investigation involved five features: size of boat (small/large), weight placed inside the boat (present/absent), sail color (red/green), sail size (small/large), and depth of water (deep/medium/shallow). A boat traveled down the canal for a timed number of seconds and reached either the blue zone (slowest), yellow zone (faster), green zone (faster), black zone (faster), or red zone (fastest). Three of the features had causal effects on outcome; sail size and sail color were noncausal.

Beth's progress in identifying the effect of the sail size feature is worthy of close examination. It illustrates that the coordination that is needed is not a linear process of gradual reconciliation between an incorrect theory and accumulating conflicting evidence. Rather, the theory itself is fluid over time, influenced at least in part by what the inquirer experiences as the fluidity of evidence, which at times seems to indicate one thing and at other times another. Beth's theories about each of the features were assessed before she began her investigations; in the course of this assessment, she exhibited conflicting strands of theory with respect to sail size. At one point she indicated that a large sail would make the boat go faster because "the wind will catch it." At another point, however, she changed her mind, saying, "No, no it doesn't. If you have the sail on there, it will still catch the breeze, and when it catches the breeze, it will still be able to run in the water with the sail."

Session 1. In constructing her first boat for a test run, Beth indicated an intent to learn about no fewer than four of the five features:

> (What are you going to find out by running this boat?) To see if the boat would make a difference with the weight, the color, the size of the sail [large], and that the water is deep.

After observing the boat reach the middle (green) zone, Beth drew this conclusion:

> (What have you found out about what makes a difference in how fast or slow the boats go?) The sail size. (How do you know?) It would be easier for the wind to catch onto it.

The second boat Beth constructed differed on all five features. The outcome posed a problem for her sail size theory, because the small sail she selected was associated with a faster outcome than the previous large sail.

Rather than acknowledge this association in the opposite direction of what she theorized, which would have meant relinquishing her initial theory, Beth reconciled theory and evidence by distorting the evidence, claiming that the two outcomes were equivalent, and resurrecting the "no difference" (noncausal) theory she had also voiced earlier.

> The sail still went fast no matter what size. (So does sail size make a difference?) No, because no matter what size it was, it caught the wind, so it will go fast. (Does the testing you've done with the boats tell you about whether the sail size makes a difference?) Yes, because with the big boat [and sail], it went pretty fast, even though the weight was in here, and with the small boat and the small sail it went pretty fast.

In her notebook Beth then wrote, "The boat went pretty fast with a small sail and a big sail."

Session 2. At the beginning of the next session, Beth indicated her intent to again investigate sail size, as well as weight, and the theory that large sails are faster than small ones reappeared.

> I found out that it didn't go further from what I said because it had a small sail. (So the small sail makes it go slower?) Yes. (How do you know?) Because this small sail went to the green flag and didn't go to the black or the red. And the last test I did with the big sail [in session 1] went past the green flag, and it almost went to the red but it didn't.

The two outcomes she compared were in fact identical, and Beth thus again distorted the evidence to fit her theory. In her notebook she recorded, "The small sail doesn't go fast."

Beth examined two more boats during this session and, with each, indicated intentions to investigate other features. In her interpretations, however, she returned each time to sail size. Regarding the first of the two, she concluded, "It went to the black because it had a big sail"; and regarding the second, she concluded:

> (So what have you found out?) The size of the sail won't be able to go as fast as the one with the big sail, because it's small and the wind won't be able to catch on to it as much as the one with the big sail. (Does any of the testing you've done with the boats tell you about whether sail size makes a difference?) Yes, when I chose the one with the big sail it went to black, and this one went only to yellow. It didn't go as fast as the one with the big sail because it's a small sail and the wind wasn't really able to catch on to the sail.

Session 3. This pattern continued during session 3; but in interpreting results for the second boat examined in this session, Beth mentioned another feature:

> (Have you found out anything else?) Yeah, when I tried the small boat it went a lot faster, and with the big boat it went a lot slower.

Beth's lack of a theoretical mechanism for explaining this effect may have impeded her recognition of the effect of boat size (which covaried perfectly with outcome in the seven boats she had constructed). At this point, however, she recorded in her notebook, "The size of the boat matters."

The final boat Beth constructed during this session, which was the first to reach the final (fastest) zone, supported the boat-size causal thesis but was markedly inconsistent with Beth's theorized sail-size effect. (A small sail is associated with the fastest outcome.) Her interpretation of the outcome suggested a fleeting recognition that boat size, not sail size, was causal:

> It came out faster than what I thought. (So what have you found out?) The size of the boat makes it go faster than the sail.

She then immediately added, however:

> The big sail makes it go faster too. (How do you know?) With the big sail it could go faster with a small boat because the wind will be able to catch on to it. (Did you find this out from the boats you ran today?) Yes. When I tried the big sail with the small boat [second boat at this session] it went to black.

Thus Beth invoked the large sail in explaining this fast outcome, but she ignored the even-faster outcome associated with the small sail [the final boat at this session].

Session 4. Beth continued during this session in a similar pattern. Her intent in constructing the final boat during this session, however, was "to see if the weight is going to make a difference or the depth of the water." She attributed the outcome of this boat to both boat size and sail size. For the first time, however, she undertook to exclude a feature as causal. Weight was noncausal, she claimed, referring to an instance in which a boat went fast with weight; and depth was noncausal, she claimed, referring to an instance in which a boat went fast in shallow water.

Session 5. At this session another important development occurred. For the first time, Beth exhibited an awareness that controlling other features might be relevant in comparing outcomes. She constructed a boat and compared it to her recollection of a session 4 boat that differed only in size and weight:

> I think size of the boat slowed this one down. (So size makes a difference?) Yes, because last week when I tried a small boat it went past the green flag, and it had the same depth of the water and the same big red sail.

She was overlooking weight, of course, which had varied across the two instances, but the concept of a controlled comparison had begun to emerge.

The final boat Beth constructed during session 5 yielded an outcome that conflicted markedly with her sail-size theory. This time, however, rather than ignore or distort the outcome, she acknowledged it and reconciled theory and evidence by revising the theory, claiming that small rather than large sail size was associated with faster outcomes.

> (Does the sail size have anything to do with it?) It makes a difference, because with the small sail it went pretty fast with the small boat. (So what have you found out?) That sometimes the small sail goes pretty faster than the big sail.

Beth did not invoke any theoretical mechanism to explain an effect in this direction. In her notebook, she wrote, "The small sail went pretty fast, than the big sail."

Session 6. Having exhibited this surprising reversal in her interpretation of sail size, Beth made no inferences regarding sail size over the next three sessions. Possibly she turned her attention away from this feature, at least in part because she could conceive of no mechanism that would explain this revised theory.

Another important development appeared, however, during this session. For the first time, Beth showed some hesitation in making inferences. When asked what she had found out, she seemed puzzled, replying, "I don't know" or "I'm not so sure." We could sense her dawning awareness that the kinds of evidence she had been generating were not readily interpretable and yet she was not sure of how else to proceed.

Session 7. During this session Beth's disequilibrium became focused and she achieved an insight. She compared two boats that differed with respect to weight and sail color:

> The weight did slow down the boat. (How do you know?) Because with the other boat I tried . . . No, it could have been the sail too, because the other

boat I tried had a green sail and it didn't have a weight in it. This one had weight in it and it was a red sail. (So what have you found out?) Nothing.

Beth immediately pursued her insight, constructing a boat with weight and a green sail. She thus had generated data that allowed her to make her first completely controlled comparison, as the basis for a noncausal inference:

When I tried a small red sail it went up to the green flag, and this one [small green sail, with size, weight, and depth unchanged] went up to the green flag. (So what have you found out?) That the color of the sail doesn't make a difference.

Session 8. During this session the preceding advance was consolidated with a repetition of the same sequence. Beth recognized that the first two boats she constructed did not allow a valid inference:

The boat does slow down with the weight in it. Or it could have been the color.

The third boat she constructed, however, was designed to resolve the indeterminacy:

(What are you going to find out?) To see if it was the weight that slowed the boat down or the color of the sail.

The result allowed Beth to draw her first valid causal inference, implicating the weight as causal.

Session 9. During this session, Beth applied her newly consolidated strategy to the sail-size feature that had been the object of so much uncertainty and that she had avoided for several sessions. She ran two boats that differed only with respect to sail size and concluded:

Sail size doesn't make a difference. (How do you know?) Because the small sail went up to the red flag and this [large] sail went up to the red flag.

By the end of nine sessions working with the boats, Beth had reached correct conclusions about the causal factors of boat size and weight and the noncausal factors of sail size and color. She never reached the correct conclusion that depth is a causal factor, having falsely excluded it during sessions 4 and 5 and thereafter ignoring it. At the end of session 9, however, in summarizing the effects of the various features and declaring depth noncausal, Beth justified this conclusion in this way:

I know this because whenever I was testing the shallow water, the boat still went the same as it did when I tested the medium and deep water.

Beth's grasp of the logic of exclusion thus appeared firm, but she demonstrated also that she could apply this logic inappropriately when the necessary evidence had not in fact been generated.

Cross-Domain Progress

Given the fluctuation observed within the boat domain, we neither expected nor observed exact session-by-session parallels across problem domains. We did observe, however, a similar evolution in Beth's work in the car domain. She advanced slightly more rapidly in the car domain, showing valid exclusion of a noncausal feature at session 5 (vs. session 7 in the boat domain). In both domains, this valid exclusion was achieved first with respect to a feature that Beth had a prior belief was noncausal; but eventually it was achieved with respect to a feature Beth initially believed was causal, which meant she had to revise her theory. Valid inclusion of a causal feature, in contrast, appeared during sessions 8 and 9 in the boat domain but was never achieved in the car domain. In sum, then, Beth showed similar, although not identical, progress across the two domains. This is crucial because it confirms that Beth was acquiring something more than information about boats and cars—a deeper knowledge having to do with how, not what, one finds out.

Promoting Development at the Meta Level

During most of Beth's inquiry, she drew on a mixture of inquiry, analysis, and inference strategies, some at or near the most effective end of the continuum and others at the least effective. This phenomenon, consistent with other findings from microgenetic research (Kuhn, 1995; Siegler, 2006), is significant because it sheds light on the nature of the developmental process. Rarely, if ever, does the process consist of an abrupt transition from one cognitive strategy to another more advanced one. Rather, multiple strategies coexist in an individual's repertory over extended periods. Development is marked by a gradual increase in frequency of use of more adequate, effective strategies and a decrease in frequency of use of less adequate ones. Moreover, microgenetic data, like Beth's, suggest that giving up old, less effective strategies poses an even more formidable challenge than acquiring new ones—a reversal of the way we typically think of development.

To explain such change, something else is needed—another level of operation distinct from the strategies themselves, which we can refer to as a *meta level* of operation. Operators at this level of the cognitive system *select* strategies to apply, in relation to task goals, and *manage* and *monitor* their application. The meta level directs the application of strategies, and feedback from this application is directed back to the meta level, as illustrated in Figure 5.5. This feedback leads to enhanced awareness of the goal and the extent to which it is being met by different strategies, as well as enhanced awareness of the strategies themselves—in particular, increased recognition of the power and the limitations associated with each. These enhancements at the meta level lead to revised strategy selection and hence changes in the distribution of usage observed at the performance level. Although Figure 5.5 suggests a discrete transition, what is implied is a continuous process, one in which the meta level both guides and is modified by the performance level. In practice, however, this mutual regulation may not always be the case because the meta level has not reached a point in its development at which it is able to maintain this high level of control, resulting in behaviors that are inconsistent across occasions and highly vulnerable to situational influence.

The important educational implication is that this meta-level (or *meta-cognitive*) development is at least as important a goal as cognitive development. If nothing has been done to influence the meta level, newly acquired behaviors will quickly disappear once the instructional context is withdrawn and students resume meta-level management of their own behavior. This limitation applies to numerous studies that have undertaken to improve thinking simply by teaching strategies ("do this"), and, if meta-level understanding is addressed at all, by assessing children's knowledge that this is what they should do. The meta-level understanding that is critical, in contrast, is *why* this is what to do and why other strategies are less effective or wrong. Indicative of fragile meta-level knowledge is the continued mixture of correct and incorrect strategies that is common following instruction.

The meta level of operation is not as directly observable as the performance level. We can attempt to assess meta-level progress—for example, by asking students to explain why it is better to apply one kind of strategy rather than another (Kuhn and Pearsall, 1998). Or we can look to less direct indicators, such as transfer of advances across different contexts (as we saw in the case of Beth's progress in the car and boat domains). Is it possible to stimulate development of the meta level directly (rather than depend entirely on the feedback from strategic performance)? How might this be done? One promising approach is social collaboration. When students find

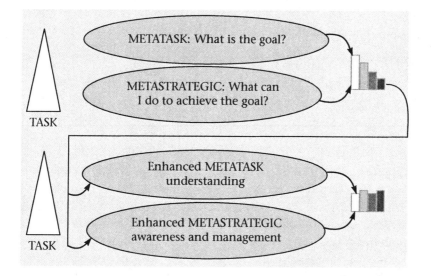

Figure 5.5. Model of strategy change. The multiple strategies in the student's repertory are represented as bars on the right side of the figure. The left-most strategy is the least effective, the right-most strategy the most effective. Heights of the bars represent the frequency of usage of a particular strategy. The developmental goal is to decrease usage of ineffective strategies and increase usage of effective ones. The figure depicts progress in achieving this goal, from an initial state in which ineffective strategies are most prevalent (upper half of figure) to a later state in which all strategies are of roughly equal frequency. The mechanism that is represented as mediating this effect is meta-level understanding.

themselves having to justify claims and strategies to one another, normally implicit meta-level cognitive processes become externalized, making them more available. I explore this idea further in later chapters.

Scaffolding Development of Inquiry Skills

If the opportunity to engage in very simple forms of inquiry over a period of months is sufficient to foster the encouraging degree of progress in the development of inquiry skills that we saw in students like Beth, we reasoned, perhaps the same opportunity could be similarly fruitful among less advantaged students in schools like the struggling school. I turn now to our efforts to explore this possibility.

Our first approach was simply to take the methods described in this chapter, which we had found fruitful in developing inquiry skills among students like those at the best-practice school, and introduce them at schools like the struggling school. In a fair number of attempts using this approach, we achieved at best limited success (Kuhn et al., 1995, 2000; Keselman, 2003). Many of these students progressed to the level at which they attended to the evidence and based inferences on comparison of two instances, although usually not consistently; but only a small minority progressed to controlled comparisons and valid inferences with a frequency any greater than once in a while. A significant proportion made no progress at all in discovering the causal structure of the database they investigated, continuing to assert, for example, the causal power of a noncausal variable, even after ten or more inquiry sessions, by drawing on fragments of evidence to support their claim while ignoring all contradictory evidence. Incorporating social collaboration was of some, but only limited, benefit, as many students simply divided the activity between them mechanically—for example, "You choose what to look at and I'll say what we found out."

It gradually became clear that the approach that had worked well among best-practice students would not suffice among academically at-risk students like those at the struggling school. Interestingly, in all but one of the struggling-school environments in which we tried our methods, an abundance of modern technology was available through various forms of external funding. Students spent time in the computer lab and were familiar with how to navigate the Internet, use search engines, communicate by email, and do basic word processing. When we introduced our inquiry software, the problem, therefore, was not a lack of familiarity with computer tools and interfaces. Students' technological know-how, to the contrary and to our surprise, appeared to be more a liability than an asset. The students seemed focused on getting the program to do what it was going to (produce outcomes), making the necessary choices that would advance the program to the next screen, and getting to the Done button that would signify completion. It proved very hard to shift students' focus to one of analysis, of understanding what determined the different outcomes. Students at schools like the struggling school are not used to being asked to apply any deep thought to a problem, and getting an assignment done is regarded as more than enough in the way of a goal. A few students made progress, but the number who did so was unacceptably small.

In the remainder of this chapter I describe the curriculum we devised in an effort to scaffold the development of inquiry skills in this population. The process of developing and implementing this curriculum afforded additional insight into the conceptual challenges these students faced. Thus, in a genre of what has been called "design-based research" (Cobb et al., 2003), at the same time that we undertook to devise an effective instructional protocol, we were able to refine our model of what is developing and needs to develop.

Music Club

Our first and most formidable challenge was to get these students to see that there was something to find out about that was real and meaningful. They needed to understand that what they were seeing on the computer screen when we presented the earthquake problem *represented* something else in the real world. It was more than a presentation that might be entertaining the first few times, or an interactive program that allowed them to create different effects.

We met this challenge by taking these computer-savvy students away from their computers entirely, at least temporarily. We assured the school staff that we would get back to the computers that they were eager to have students use, and we also managed to convince them that the topic of our activity for the students—a music club offering mail-order sale of CDs—was of educational value and could serve as a means of developing inquiry skills, a goal that all of the staff endorsed.

Session 1. Students were introduced to the following scenario:

> We're going to work as advisers to a music club. Most music clubs send cata-
> logs to their members about once a month. Each catalog offers members a
> lot of different kinds of music to choose from. Members can order the CDs
> they want by mailing in an order card. Then the club sends them the CDs
> and they pay the club. That's how music clubs make money. The more
> CDs the club sells, the more money it makes.
>
> One thing the club directors have found out is that changing certain
> things about the catalogs can affect how many CDs they sell. Some kinds of
> catalogs sell more CDs than others. And they've also found out that they get
> different results in different parts of the country. So they've been spending a
> lot of time trying out different features of the catalogs in different cities.
> They want to find out how these features affect their sales.

Students worked in groups of six to eight, with two adult coaches who later split the group into two subgroups of three to four. Displaying a large posterboard with removable Velcro attachments, the coach initially introduced only two variable features:

> Let's start by looking at two features they tried out in their mailings in New
> York City. One is the kind of *illustration*. They've tried illustrating the pic-
> tures of CDs in the catalog in two different ways—either with pictures of the

CD covers or with pictures of the artists who play or sing the music. Another feature is the format of the catalog. They've tried two different kinds of formats of the catalog—sometimes a booklet and other times a foldout.

Each of the features was depicted and labeled on the posterboard, together with two catalogs attached below the feature label depicting the two levels of that feature. Beneath *illustration,* in other words, appeared (attached by Velcro) an actual catalog with pictures of CD covers and next to it a catalog with pictures of artists. Beneath *format* appeared a catalog in booklet format and another catalog in foldout format.

The coach proposed, "Let's think about format first—booklet or foldout." He then asked, "Do you think the foldout or booklet would give them better sales?" Students offered their opinions and, on that basis, were split into two groups: those who theorized that the foldout would generate better sales and those who theorized that the booklet would generate better sales. (Students rarely expressed a theory of no difference.) Each group was asked to discuss and then present reasons for their positions. The coach summed up:

> Well you have good ideas, but you obviously don't agree. How can we find out? Luckily we have some records that show what kinds of sales they get in New York City with each type of format, booklet and foldout.

The "booklet" and "foldout" groups separated at this point to look at the records within their respective groups. The coach of each group introduced two catalogs to his group, displaying and labeling them as he placed them on a new posterboard. One was in booklet form with artist illustrations. The other, placed diagonally to the right and beneath it, was in foldout form with CD-cover illustrations. Velcro strips displaying the sales outcomes were then placed beneath each catalog—"GOOD" beneath the booklet/artist catalog and "FAIR" beneath the foldout/CD-cover catalog. The coach then facilitated discussion of these sales records, drawing on these questions:

> What do you think? What does it show? How do they compare? Which one is better? What could be making this one better than that one?

Once these questions were addressed and the students had made the effort to interpret the results, the coach asked the following key question:

> Is there anything else different about the two you're comparing that could be causing the difference you're seeing?

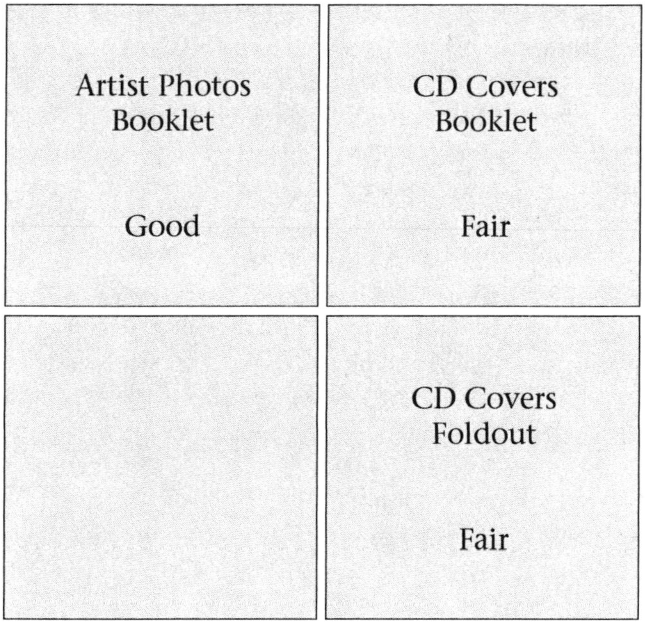

Artist Photos Booklet Good	CD Covers Booklet Fair
	CD Covers Foldout Fair

Figure 5.6. Initial phase of music-club inquiry activity.

Following discussion of this possibility, the coach asked:

Is there any other kind of catalog we could look at to see for sure?

After discussion of possible comparisons, the group settled on a third catalog to examine, and the coach displayed it, although initially without any sales outcome. He asked the group to identify which of the two catalogs already on the board the new catalog should be compared to, to see whether format made a difference. Once the group decided, he added an outcome for the new catalog (Figure 5.6) and asked the students to draw conclusions. At the end of this discussion, he repeated the key question:

Is there anything else different about the two you're comparing that could be causing the difference you're seeing?

This time, students were able to answer no and, in the case depicted in Figure 5.6, drew the conclusion that format had no effect on sales. Finally, the two subgroups (who held contrasting initial theories) reassembled and a spokesperson from each subgroup reported to the full group on the subgroup's conclusion and the evidence to support it.

Sessions 2–12. Each of the remaining sessions is designed to incorporate a conceptual advance, sometimes only a fairly small one, relative to the preceding session, while other dimensions of the inquiry setting remained the same. These sessions are summarized in Box 5.1 by number and by the city being investigated. As Box 5.1 shows, the complexity of the multivariable causal structure increases gradually with respect to the number of variable features and the number of causal features present. In addition, students transition gradually from real, physically present objects (the catalogs) to symbolic representations of them.

Increasing the number of variable features increases the cognitive challenge of identifying an appropriate comparison to assess the effect of any individual feature. Increasing the number of causal features from one to two or more necessitates students' developing facility in an additive causal model, one in which identifying a causal effect of one variable is recognized as leaving open the causal status of other variables. In addition, students must grapple, at each level of complexity, with the more fundamental conceptualization of variables, outcomes, and causality. A common error, for example, continues to be the confusion of variable and variable level, as when a student claims that the foldout makes a difference to the outcome but the booklet does not.

Transition to self-directed inquiry. In session 13, students were introduced to the self-directed inquiry format of the earthquake inquiry program and allowed to experiment with it. They were not given any more instruction in how to proceed than the program itself provides. They were, however, encouraged to see the parallel between this inquiry activity and the music club project they had been working on.

Progress of Students from the Struggling School

A group of sixth-grade students at the struggling school, as well as two groups of sixth graders from a comparable neighboring school, participated in the music club inquiry activity. Subsequent assessment of their inquiry skills, based on the earthquake and avalanche inquiry programs, showed that, relative to a comparison group who did not participate, almost all of these students—over 90 percent—made substantial progress. Almost all based their inferences of causality and noncausality not only on empirical evidence they selected to examine but on appropriate comparisons designed to answer well-formed questions (about the effects of individual features), with these comparisons controlled so as to eliminate alternative hypotheses.

Box 5.1 _____

SUMMARY OF SESSIONS 2–12 IN SCAFFOLDED INQUIRY PROGRAM

2. LOS ANGELES

The same two features are presented (format and illustration).

One feature is causal and one is not.

Advance: The causal feature is changed to format and the noncausal feature to illustration.

Conceptual goal: Understanding that the causal status of a feature may vary in different contexts.

3. ORLANDO

Two features are presented (color and illustration).

One feature is causal and one is not.

Advance: A new feature is introduced.

Conceptual goal: Generalization of the two-feature structure across different feature content.

4. CHICAGO

Two features are presented (number of CDs in catalog and color).

One feature is causal and one is not.

Advance: Students are asked to prepare a claim sheet to support their claim.

Conceptual goal: Making explicit the connection between a claim and supporting evidence.

5. DALLAS

Two features are presented (number and format).

Advance: Both features are causal.

Conceptual goal: Developing facility in a model of multivariable additive causality.

6. PHILADELPHIA

Two features are presented (color and format).

Both features are causal.

Advance: A computerized depiction of catalog features is substituted for the actual catalogs. (See Figure 5.7.)

Conceptual goal: Representing features and feature levels symbolically.

7. SEATTLE

Two features are presented (number and illustration).

One feature is causal and one is not.

Advance: No overlap of features or of causal structure from previous session.

Conceptual goal: Further practice and generalization of reasoning with symbolic entities.

8. ATLANTA

Advance: Three features are presented (color, illustration, and number). (See Figure 5.8.)

To limit complexity, only one feature is causal.

To limit complexity, only two cases are examined and comparison for only one feature is made.

Conceptual goal: Three-dimensional representation of the presence of three features.

9. HOUSTON

Three features are presented (color, illustration, and number).

To limit complexity, only one feature is causal.

Advance: Four cases are examined and comparisons made for all three features.

Conceptual goal: Developing facility in coordinating feature being investigated with appropriate comparison.

10. SAN ANTONIO

Three features are presented (color, illustration, and number).

Advance: Two features are causal and one is not.

Conceptual goal: Further developing facility in a model of multivariable additive causality.

11. PHOENIX

Three features are presented (color, format, and illustration).

Two features are causal and one is not.

Advance: Transition from cube to more general tree structure, allowing unlimited number of features to be represented.

Conceptual goal: Generalized representation of multivariable additive causality.

12. BALTIMORE

Two features are causal and two are not.

Advance: Four features are presented (color, format, illustration, and number).

Conceptual goal: Further developing facility in a model of multivariable additive causality.

Empowering All Students to Inquire and Learn

Students like those at the struggling school may need more support to develop the skills that students like those at the best-practice school are able to develop merely through practice. But there is no evidence to suggest that such students cannot develop them, given a suitable context, within a time frame similar to that observed among their more advantaged peers.

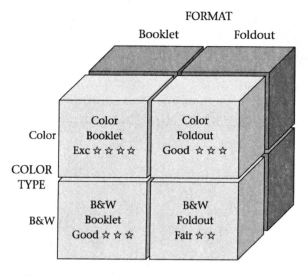

Figure 5.7. Symbolic depiction of catalog features.

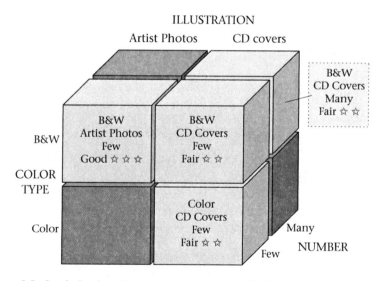

Figure 5.8. Symbolic depiction of catalog features with three features represented.

It is worth emphasizing this fact, given the discontinuity between the kind of thinking that we asked struggling-school students to engage in and the cognitive demands of their school environment. I observed a few individual exceptions at the struggling school, when a teacher, for example, engaged a student in a sustained discussion about a topic; but for the most part these students were not challenged to think intently or deeply about anything during a typical school day. An intuitive "first-thought" response was usually sufficient to satisfy most demands. These students were accustomed to being asked to comply with instructions regarding what to do. They were less accustomed to being asked to think about and decide what to do.

Some may object that questions of the sort posed in the music club activity hardly qualify as requiring deep-level thinking about significant matters. Modern life is laden with complex problems and issues of great significance—capital punishment is one example—that require rich, nuanced thinking. Ought we to be asking students to devote time to topics as seemingly simplistic and insignificant as these?

The next section of the book—Part III—examines middle-school students engaged in extended discussions of capital punishment, in the context of a program to support the development of argument skills. In that context, I address how students think about and debate such a topic and how their cognitive skills develop as a result. In the conclusion of this chapter, it bears emphasis that what we were asking students to do in the music club inquiry activity was far from trivial. Simplistic as the content may seem, and as straightforward as the cognitive skills themselves may seem to the sophisticated observer, these are fundamental skills that need to develop as a foundation for more sophisticated, content-rich forms of inquiry.

Once the basic forms of coordination of theory and evidence that these skills entail have become "second nature" to students, they will be secure in moving on to the more complex forms of evidence-theory coordination that await them in any of the fields of endeavor in which they choose to inquire. Such contexts are likely to be ones in which variables assume levels more complex than a simple dichotomy; in which outcomes are probabilistic instead of certain, due to the influence of unknown, hence uncontrollable, factors; in which variables interact with one another in complex ways; and in which a variable functions as both cause and effect in a larger constellation of interacting factors.

The inquiry contexts described in this chapter lack all of these forms of structural complexity. Neither do they undertake to enrich students' scientific understanding of particular phenomena within the physical or social world. Nor do they fit neatly into any curriculum subject area. Nonetheless, I make the case here that they are worthy of serious engagement by students and careful examination by educators. In the contexts that have been described in this chapter, students are not taught rules or strategies of how to conduct inquiry. They are engaged and guided in the very simple practice of it, which allows them to gain their own sense of the power it affords.

Educators commonly see one of their major roles as helping students to acquire broader and deeper understandings of the physical and social world around them. Yet it is the *capacity to advance these understandings* that is involved in developing skills of inquiry. Doing so is at least as important as an educational goal.

ARGUMENT | III

Just about everyone, we noted—education theorists, teachers, parents, even students—is enthusiastic about inquiry as a worthy educational activity. Becoming an independent learner is an objective hard to be against. Argument doesn't get the same immediately enthusiastic reception. Its value is less clear. Inquiry yields new knowledge, new understanding. The fruits of argument are less apparent.

Most middle- and high-school teachers do say that it is important for students to engage in discussion and that they try to make time for it in their classrooms. Yet they have even less to turn to in the way of resources than do teachers wishing to bring inquiry into their classrooms. Teachers are largely on their own in devising ways to promote discussion and debate, to assess whether the discussions that occur in their classrooms are productive, and, if not, to figure out how they might be improved. And, as high-stakes tests play an ever-increasing role in assessing student outcomes, they are uncertain how much time they ought to be devoting to it.

Nor is it even clear what counts as argument. Argument is fine, people may feel, as long as it supports conclusions they like. Otherwise, something's gone wrong and it's not to be trusted. Is this the extent of interest in argument, or do we want students to become skilled in authentic argument—the kind whose outcome is not known in advance?

Argument can assume either an interior, individual form, as when one argues with oneself or formulates a line of reasoning to support a claim (argument as a product), or an exterior, social form, when two or more people engage in the process of arguing with one another (argument as a process). Although distinct, these two forms of argument are closely related (Billig, 1987; Kuhn, 1991) and entail a similar (though not identical) set of skills.

In this and the next two chapters, I make the case that developing skills of argument is, like inquiry, valuable education for life. Students need not only to argue but also to learn to argue well. Like inquiry, argument has the virtue of revealing its value and power in the course of being practiced. It

113

doesn't need to be sold in any other way, as a means to achieving some different end. And, unlike inquiry, as we shall see, it has the advantage of its roots in everyday conversation.

Although teachers do not have a great deal to go on in knowing how best to develop their students' argument skills, there is no shortage of arguments as to why they should do so. The next section examines the numerous benefits that have been attributed to partaking in argument.

What Does Argument Accomplish?

One way to think of argument is as a form of inquiry. When engaged collectively, as they are much of the time in both work and private life, people attempt to solve a problem, resolve an issue, or make a decision through discourse with one another. Whether initially they oppose one another or see things similarly, in the course of discussion they identify alternatives and generate and weigh reasons for and against them. Skilled argument moves in some direction and has goals of its own, above and beyond the roles of individual participants (Bereiter, 2002). Yet the thinking of individual participants is enriched by it. Both individually and collectively, then, people advance their interests and objectives through argument, and in the process enhance their knowledge. Without the ability to argue, an individual's potential to contribute to the collective welfare would be diminished.

Arguing Together and Alone

Research has demonstrated the superiority of collaborative over individual reasoning and problem solving (Kuhn, 2001; Moshman and Geil, 1998; Resnick, Levine, and Teasley, 1991; Schwarz, Newman, and Biezuner, 2000). Compared to thinking alone, people make more progress, and make it more quickly, if they are thinking collaboratively, even when none of them initially has the right approach. And so, if there is an issue to resolve or problem to solve, we would prefer, whenever possible, to have the proverbial two—or three or twelve—heads address it, rather than just one. Indeed, the jury system in democratic societies rests on exactly this premise. It is not surprising that cultures have evolved in such a way that people have learned to work together, to pool intellectual as well as material resources.

What are the implications for the individual? Do individuals contribute their intellectual resources to the group at personal cost or at personal gain? At a minimum, argumentive discourse provides the individual with exposure to others' ideas and perspectives. It also aids in the expression and development of one's own ideas, through the process of communicating them to others. This benefit occurs even when the listener provides no reaction. If

I go into a room with an orangutan to share some new ideas, the orangutan just sits and eats its banana, but I come out of the room clearer about my ideas.

What about longer-term, more enduring benefits? Here we find more strong claims for the value of argument. Engaging in argumentive discourse is thought to enhance individual thinking competencies by forcing normally covert, meta-level questions—How do you know? What makes you say that? Are there any other possibilities?—out into the open. Through participating in such discourse, students acquire the skills and values that lead them to pose the same questions to themselves (Olson and Astington, 1993). The result is enhanced monitoring and management of their own thinking.

We can go further, as have numerous authors (Billig, 1987; Graff, 2003; Kuhn, 1991), and claim that participation in argumentive discourse directly supports individual argument in support of a claim, because the latter contains within it the implicit structure of a full dialogic (social) argument—in other words, claim, counterclaim, and arguments for and against each. In the absence of a counterclaim, a claim scarcely needs supporting. Participating in dialogic argument should thus enhance the ability to make effective individual (nondialogic) arguments for or against a claim, as well as to evaluate the individual arguments made by others. Evidence described in Chapter 8 shows this to be the case.

Graff (2003) goes still further in claiming that dialogic argument scaffolds the development of students' skills in traditional expository writing. The standard writing assignment—state a thesis and support it—Graff says, fails to reproduce the conditions of real-world (dialogic) argument. In the absence of a physically present interlocutor, the student takes the writing task to be one of stringing together a sequence of true statements, avoiding the complication of stating anything that might not be true. The result is often a communication in which both reader and writer are left uncertain as to why the argument needs to be made at all. Who would claim otherwise? If students plant a "naysayer"—an imaginary opponent—in their written arguments, Graff suggests, as a scaffold for the missing interlocutor, their essays become more like authentic arguments and more meaningful. In sum, then, discourse, even if implicit, aids in articulating an individual point of view.

What Is Worth Arguing About?

Given all of the apparent benefits, there would seem little question that students ought to spend time arguing. How do we get them engaged in it? Here, it would appear we have something already on our side, for young people argue every day. Is this music group worth listening to? Why can't this kind of clothing be worn to school? Why do I have to be back so early? How can we get this teacher to loosen up? The arguments may not be well formed or expressed. They may leave more implicit than is explicit. But they are arguments, nonetheless. As educators, our goal is twofold: to improve the quality of students' arguments and to expand the range of topics they regard as worth arguing about. Yet their own arguments about everyday matters offer a valuable point of entry. If a student has a claim he or she genuinely cares about and would like to see respected, we have already come a long way toward the goal. We can then work to help the student situate the claim in a framework of alternatives and evidence and to enter the claim into the arena of debate.

Yet, teachers are likely to be uncertain about what classroom debate should accomplish. As a result, they tend not to be comfortable devoting classroom time to discussion of "trivial" topics like music groups or even dress codes. At least students should be airing their views on something important, a teacher might think, a topic that will contribute to their education. Hence, we are more likely to observe a classroom debate on the merits of the United Nations or the Declaration of Independence—topics debated in Ms. B's and Mrs. O's classrooms. Such topics have the drawback of being very far from middle-school students' personal experience, but their appeal to teachers lies in the expectation that students may actually learn something about an important topic, in addition to the experience they gain in debate.

Teachers' concern to ensure that students "learn something" is fed, perhaps, by their uncertainty as to what discussion itself has to teach them. A possibility to consider is that teachers would be more comfortable with a wider range of discussion topics—some "academic" and some not—to the extent that they had a clearer sense of the goals to which these discussions should aspire.

Arguing Versus Arguing Well

If engaging students in discussion and debate is such a good idea on so many different grounds, why are so many teachers ambivalent about doing it and uncertain about whether they are doing it well? The answer I propose parallels the one proposed earlier for inquiry skills. Teachers confront the substantial uncharted terrain between engaging in the activity and developing the skills. Although its origins lie in everyday conversation, effective argument does not emerge "naturally," any more than does effective inquiry. Missing, then, is a cognitive roadmap of the skills that need to develop.

As with inquiry, teachers need such a roadmap if they are to plan and implement effective instruction and assess its success. Without it, how do they know whether the kinds of activities in which they engage students are successful in advancing the desired skills? How do they know what to expect and look for? With respect to debate, is the object merely to give students the opportunity to express themselves and hear one another's ideas? Or is something more expected to happen? In the absence of well-defined goals, the activities are at high risk of being crowded out of the classroom agenda by other, more pressing demands and goals.

The next chapters offer such a roadmap, one I claim is essential if developing argument skills is to be taken seriously as an educational goal. Like the roadmap of inquiry skills, it is far from complete or definitive. Yet it suggests the directions in which argument skills develop and identifies guideposts that define the path. Argument is ubiquitous in people's lives, and the case is compelling that students need to learn to argue well, that doing so is critical education for life. Yet relatively little attention has been paid to the path from arguing to arguing well that we would like to see students navigate.

A further obstacle that teachers face in seeking to develop students' argument skills has more to do with the culture in which young people grow up today, one in which *what* one thinks is more important than *why* and reasoned argument is not highly valued in much of American culture. I return to this obstacle at the end of the chapter. First, we turn again to observations of the Social Studies classrooms in the struggling school and best-practice school. What sorts of activities did Ms. B. and Mrs. O introduce for engaging students in argumentive discourse? How effective were these activities and how could they become more effective?

Developing Argument Skills at the Struggling School

Given the emphasis at the struggling school on "basic skills" and their assessment via standardized tests, I was surprised and heartened to learn that Ms. B included debate in her lesson plans. She described three debates her eighth-grade students had engaged in during the year, the first on whether Columbus should have won the support of Spain, the second on whether the Fourth Amendment to the U.S. Constitution barred schools from searching student lockers, and the third on whether the United Nations should disband. The third debate I observed.

Also heartening was the way in which Ms. B spoke about her goals with respect to these activities. Her major goal, she said, was for students to be able to justify their opinions. When they just stated an opinion, they learned how weak it sounded. They learned that opinions are not meaningful without something to back them up. Other goals, Ms. B said, were for students to become comfortable speaking to a group and to develop listening skills. They had to learn to listen and wait until the other person completed speaking, she said, rather than jumping in without listening.

The first goal Ms. B mentions comes very close to the first important step in developing argument skills—coming to appreciate that opinions require reasons to support them (see Chapter 8). Although it seems only a small step on the way to skilled argument, we cannot assume that the average middle schooler has already achieved this recognition. I was thus optimistic that I might see progress taking place in this respect in the debate activities in Ms. B's classroom.

In preparation for the U.N. debate, Ms. B assigned students to either a pro team (representing the position that the U.N. is a valuable organization) or a con team (representing the position that the U.N. is not effective and should disband). Students did not have a voice in their team assignments. She then gave the entire class an in-class assignment to write an essay containing three reasons supporting their assigned position. Students were not permitted to collaborate on this assignment. These essays were collected and read by Ms. B and returned for correction if the essay did not contain at least three reasons. Students showed no more interest in this assignment than they did in most of their in-class assignments, and off-task behavior during the class period was high. Some students complained that they did not know any reasons, and Ms. B circulated around the room during part of the period offering individual help and encouragement.

The class atmosphere was notably different during the next class period, when the debate itself took place. The furniture was rearranged from the usual front-facing rows of desks into two long rows facing one another, with the pro team instructed to sit in one row and the con team in the other. Students were quieter than usual, with a sense of anticipation, while Ms. B presented instructions for the debate. Once it began, Ms. B called on students to speak, alternating pro and con sides. When called on, Ms. B instructed, a speaker was to either respond to the speaker from the opposing side, or introduce a new argument. One point would be awarded for either. If a student interrupted a speaker on either team or spoke without being called on, the student's team would have one point deducted from their score.

Students remained uncharacteristically attentive as the debate began, with the usual noise level much diminished. There was a sense that something significant was going on, in contrast to the typical class period. Although no tangible reward was being offered, students appeared highly motivated to have their side win. Ms. B had returned students' earlier essays and instructed students to keep these in front of them as a resource during the debate. In discussing their performance later, she expressed disappointment that they did not make more use of the essays and failed to voice during the debate many of the points they had included in their essays. When it was their turn to speak, most students introduced a new idea, rather than responding to anything said previously. Rarely did students make any acknowledgment of statements made by speakers on the opposing side. They typically acknowledged statements by speakers on their own side by clapping.

Although the argumentive skill level was not high, and students' very limited knowledge about the topic meant that the same few ideas tended to be repeated, I was left sharing the students' sense that something important was happening during this class period. Students were engaged and attuned to a shared activity in a way that was not typical during other class periods. One factor certainly was the competitive one—one team was going to win and the other lose. But beyond that, I think, was the satisfaction most of these students derived from being able to express an opinion and be listened to, in a context that was officially sanctioned—they were not "talking out of turn," as was usually the case whenever they expressed themselves during class time. Most of the school day for these students was about being quiet, following instructions, and complying with demands. Rarely, in their school lives, and most likely in their lives outside of school, did they have the experience of expressing a significant idea and being listened to and taken seriously.

At the same time, significant weaknesses were evident in this activity as a vehicle for the development of cognitive skills. Before addressing them, I turn to Mrs. O's classroom at the best-practice school to describe how a parallel activity was carried out there.

Developing Argument Skills at the Best-Practice School

Oral presentations have become familiar classroom activities to students at the best-practice school by the time they reach middle school. In one such activity, pairs of students chose a colonial settlement to "sell back" to Britain as a desirable community in a presentation to the rest of the class (see Chapter 3). Debate activities were referred to as "simulations" (of an authentic debate, usually from a particular historical period) and took place frequently in English and Social Studies classes in middle school and continuing throughout high school.

The simulation I observed in Mrs. O's seventh-grade Social Studies class extended over two class periods and was introduced to students as a simulation of the second Continental Congress. The time had come, Mrs. O explained, for the colonialists to decide what to do. Should they sever their ties to Britain and declare independence, or should they remain loyal to the mother country? The class was divided arbitrarily into two teams, one representing the revolutionaries and the other the loyalists. Mrs. O's instruction to the teams was to spend the first class period meeting as a team and coming up with all of the arguments they could to support their position. She suggested as sources assignments C, E, and F in their notebooks, but also instructed students to "use your brains." She proposed the analogy of parent and child as a way to think about the issue.

Furniture was rearranged to form two long narrow tables, with each team seated around their own table. At the table I observed, girls grouped themselves at one end and boys at the other. As the teams began their work, Mrs. O instructed, "Let's everybody look for information and then share it. Be sure to back up what you're saying." She also suggested that one person on the team be selected as scribe to write down any good ideas, although this was not what I observed happen.

During the twenty minutes of the period that was left for students to begin work, I observed little conversation between students. Instead, students worked individually, looking through notes and compiling their own lists of points to support their team's position. Mrs. O circulated during this time, talking with individual students and giving them encouragement. "That's good; write that down," she said several times to different students. Occasionally, a student volunteered, "I have an idea." Boys were more likely than girls to elicit a response from their peers; but for the most part, students did not respond and merely kept working on their own lists. Proposals were more often directed to the teacher, when she was available, than to other students. At one point, a boy announced aloud, "Okay, I think I have enough to make my point." As the period came to a close, Mrs. O told students that they would get more ideas in that night's reading assignment.

The next day, the day of the simulation, tables were arranged in a single long row, with the loyalists seated in a row along one side and the revolutionaries along the other side facing them. Mrs. O announced some rules—for example, that no one would have a second turn to speak until every team member had spoken once. She then opened the debate by calling on a member of one team to make an argument for his side. When he had finished, she called on someone from the opposing team to respond, and continued in this fashion, alternating speakers from the two teams until everyone had had a turn. In calling on a new speaker, Mrs. O several times prompted the speaker to "reply to the person who has just spoken." Nonetheless, like students in Ms. B's class, the students tended to look at the teacher while they spoke, rather than at any of their classmates. They also tended to draw on their prepared notes in choosing what to say. And even in this respect, they evidenced some uncertainty about how to proceed. One student asked, for example, "Should we argue or just give out facts?"

The overall structure of the students' activity was thus not that different from what I observed in Ms. B's class, even though Mrs. O's students were more articulate and had much more factual information available. Like Ms. B's students, they expressed what they had worked out to say when their turns came. But there was even less a sense than there was in Ms. B's classroom of students engaging in discourse with one another. Even a five-minute break that Mrs. O called midway through the debate for team members to confer with one another did not become an occasion for student-to-student talk. Instead, it became an opportunity for one or two students to consult with Mrs. O about an idea, while other students did little but wait.

One difference between the two classes did stand out. The air of competition apparent in Ms. B's class was absent in Mrs. O's class. Mrs. O did not declare a winning team and her students seemed to be aware that they would be evaluated based on their individual contributions, not on the standing of their team relative to the opposing team.

At the end of the debate, Mrs. O made a five-minute presentation that made it clearer to students what they were expected to take away from the activity. On the blackboard she had earlier written two lists labeled "long-term issues" and "short-term issues." They contained items such as "the Proclamation of 1763" and "the Sugar Act of 1764." Mrs. O opened her summary by asking the class, "How much of the stuff on the board have we covered today?" In studying for the upcoming exam, she advised students to compare their notes from the simulation with what appeared on the board. She also suggested they write down in their notes anything that they didn't get a chance to say during the class period.

Mrs. O had very ambitious knowledge goals for her class. In her view, the students needed to master a great deal of factual material. She saw the simulation activity as an effective way of reviewing that material and helping students to organize and master it. Like the cause-and-effect framework discussed in Chapter 3, Mrs. O used the discourse framework not as a significant object of development in its own right but rather as a tool for information management and retention. She made this explicit to the students, and they seemed to accept it as the purpose of the activity.

Ms. B's knowledge goals were much less ambitious, leaving her freer to concentrate on the process. Both teachers, nonetheless, seem attuned to some of the potential dividends of the process students are engaged in. Getting students engaged in making claims and supporting them in dialog with their peers seems a valuable thing to be doing. Students are active. They gain experience in expressing themselves clearly and concisely. And they learn to listen to what others have to say. The question we now turn our attention to is what more such activities have the potential to do.

Talking to One Another

Teachers conducting classroom discussions commonly make one of two mistakes. One of them is to allow the activity to lapse into nothing but consecutive self-expression, first on the part of one student, then another. It does not matter much what each student says, and no student need listen to another. In this worst-case scenario, the only attention a student pays to the previous speaker is to wait to observe a signal that this speaker is about to finish, so that he or she can begin. As long as everyone gets their share of turns to speak and no one speaks too long, there is a wealth of opportunity for self-expression. Yet, no further purpose is fulfilled. There is no continuity, no direction, no sequence to the discussion. Nor is there any particular role for the teacher to play except the procedural one of ensuring that the turn-taking norms are followed.

The other mistake teachers make is to retain tight control of the activity so as to ensure that the content of what is said meets the teacher's understanding of what needs to be covered. The teacher calls on students successively; and if a student begins to veer off track, the teacher steers him or her back, if necessary with a more specific question ("let me ask you this"). Or the teacher may simply go on to another student—a tactic even the best teachers are guilty of—until some student gives the response the teacher is seeking.

Although Mrs. O let students know during her end-of-class summary the important points that had been covered, she did not resort to teacher-controlled discussion during the debate itself. Neither Mrs. O nor Ms. B said much during the debate except to call on students to speak. Both teachers, however, succumbed to a less blatant version of teacher control. They allowed the direction of students' conversation to flow from student to

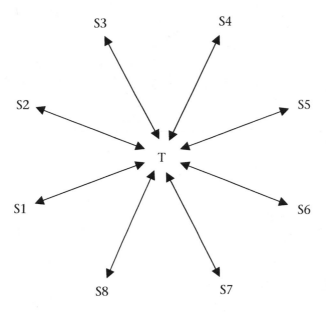

Figure 6.1. Self-expression and teacher-controlled modes of classroom discussion.

teacher. In neither classroom did students direct their remarks to one another. This communication pattern worked against the continuity and sequence characteristic of genuine discourse. Each student's utterance was a new, and isolated, communication to the teacher. As a result, the other risk—of the activity consisting of nothing more than opportunities for self-expression—escalated.

To Whom Am I Speaking?

In both the self-expression and teacher-controlled discussion modes, the same model of communication prevails. All talk is directed to the teacher (Figure 6.1). The most a student can hope for in the way of response is approval from the teacher for what he or she has said, before it becomes another student's turn to speak. Whether or not the teacher communicates it explicitly to students, the teacher's own behavior models the norm that we must be respectful of others' ideas, and students are usually quick to pick it up. Hence, students rarely experience any strong reactions to the statements they make in classroom discussion. Instead, the typical response is the one that teachers so often rely on when they can think of nothing else to say before moving on to another student: "That's an interesting idea."

This form of communication stands in striking contrast to the discourse

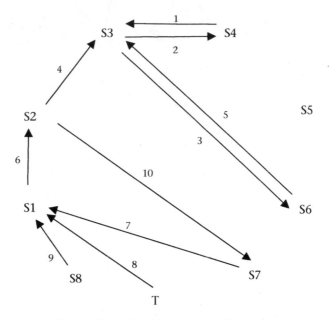

Figure 6.2. Authentic classroom discourse.

students engage in as soon as they leave the classroom and enter the school-yard. One student makes a claim, another challenges it, and others may join in (Figure 6.2); strict reciprocity between any pair of participants is not expected, but still a speaker addresses the claim that has just been made, with the goal of reaching a resolution. Such a discussion has a life that goes beyond the role of individual participants. If interest is not keen enough to maintain the discussion, it evolves to a new topic or terminates. Rarely do participants continue to talk *about* the topic without talking *to* one another.

Does this model need to become the norm for classroom discussion? Students have plenty of opportunity for social interaction outside of school. Is it critical that they talk to one another in the classroom? The single most important claim I make in this chapter is that indeed it is—that this is the one feature of classroom discussion that must be captured and preserved above any others. Why?

The answer, in simplest terms, is that the central purpose of the activity is to develop students' argument skills and that these skills are, in essence, dialogic. Their roots lie in ordinary conversation between two speakers. It is from these roots in everyday experience that argument skills develop.

In even the simplest of everyday conversations, certain assumptions hold—that one speaker speaks *to* the other, with the expectation that the other person will listen, that the listener will construct and communicate a reply that is shaped by what the listener has understood the speaker to say, and that the first speaker will then do the same, and that this process will continue for as long as the conversation lasts. Except in the case of young children, whom Piaget (1926) described as engaging in "collective mono- logs," conversation is unlikely to continue if these assumptions are violated. We speak to people with the expectation that they will understand and re- spond to what we've said. Otherwise, we are unlikely to bother.

It is essential, then, that students participate in authentic conversations as the primary context in which to develop argument skills. Like all authentic conversations, these social exchanges must have a topic, a purpose, a direc- tion, and a goal. They can begin at an early age, because of their roots in everyday experience, and gradually become more focused, extensive, and skilled. Only with extended experience in engaging in these exchanges modeled on everyday conversation can we expect students to develop the skills and facility that will allow them to participate effectively in dialogic arguments, as well as to interiorize dialogic exchanges into their own indi vidual arguments for or against a claim.

I thus propose everyday dialog about a disputed claim as a template for the development of students' argument skills. I devote the next two chap- ters to examining the nature of these skills and the patterns of their devel- opment. These are the skills that educators should be seeking to develop when they engage students in discourse-based activities. The more that is understood about what these skills are and how they develop, the more ef- fective such activities have the potential to become.

Why Talk About This?

The next two chapters look closely at the arguments of middle-school stu- dents about a social issue of genuine concern in contemporary society—the merits of capital punishment. This topic is one of broad and enduring inter- est in contrast to, say, the merits of a particular set of school rules that stu- dents, at that particular school and in the time period when those rules were enforced, might debate. In the latter type of argument, students face the additional challenge of disentangling their own self-interest from their reasoning (a not insignificant challenge, research has shown), but this sort of "local" topic also has the disadvantage of tying observations of students' performance to a very specific context, making it difficult to make compari- sons across contexts.

The capital punishment topic, compared to numerous other social issues, also has the advantage of having associated with it a large number and variety of arguments supporting both pro and con positions, making it possible for rich debate to develop. In addition, the topic is one that even middle-school students feel entitled to have opinions on and competent to debate—unlike, say, environmental pollution, a topic in which technical knowledge figures more prominently.

Two further features of the topic are at least as critical. First, students can readily appreciate that something important—literally, people's lives—is at stake. For this reason, it is easier for them to see a point to the debate, to feel it is worth engaging, than with an historical topic such as whether the revolutionaries ought to have declared independence (Mrs. O's class) or even a contemporary topic like abolition of the U.N. (which Ms. B's students seemed to regard as an abstraction of little practical consequence to anyone).

Second, and finally, students can relate the issue to an individual person's experience and life. Is a particular individual innocent or guilty, what led that person to commit the crime, should that person live or die, how will others be affected by the decision? All of these questions are at the forefront of students' thinking and debate. Many other social issues, by comparison, remain safely in the realm of abstraction, only indirectly connected to individual human experience.

On the negative side, however, classroom teachers and education theorists alike question the risks associated with bringing such value-laden topics into the classroom. Can we preserve each student's right to have his or her ideas respected while exposing students to the possibly conflicting values of their classmates? The argument has now been made by a number of contemporary education theorists that, to the contrary, the risk lies in not doing so. Engaging students in debate about serious, value-laden issues provides a way to transcend disputes over whose values should prevail in the classroom. By involving students in discussions of the value controversies themselves, they are able to understand what the debates are about—whether the issue is deciding which authors merit inclusion on the reading list or the rights of gun owners—and to participate in the discourse surrounding them (Graff, 1992; Simon, 2001). Getting students deeply involved with ideas themselves, Graff (1992) exclaims, is far more important than endless debate about which particular ideas they should or should not be exposed to. Engaging one's views in the arena of discourse becomes a more important value than protecting those views from challenge. I return to this claim at the conclusion of the chapter.

Valuing Argument

Students need to make meaning of what they do in school, and inquiry is an activity that comes to make sense as it is engaged (see Chapter 3). Students discover for themselves how and why it is important. Argument has the advantage of its tie to the already familiar activity of everyday conversation. Yet its value is less immediately apparent. Authentic inquiry rests on identifying a question; finding answers to that question gives the activity its purpose and meaning. No such clear outcome is visible in the case of argument.

What Is the Point?

Argument nonetheless can have—indeed, must have—the same sense of purpose as does inquiry, a sense that allows those who engage in it to experience and appreciate for themselves its value. We can undertake to make teachers aware of all of the cognitive benefits that have been documented to accrue from engaging students in argumentive discourse, reassuring them that classroom discussion is not a waste of time. But students need to discover this value for themselves. They cannot simply be told. Ultimately, students must come to see argument not only as purposeful and fruitful, but also as yielding the same potential dividend as does inquiry: richer understanding, individually and collectively. Argument, like inquiry, is a path to knowing.

What does it take for this to happen? First and foremost, students must be able to create authentic conversations to argue in. What makes argument authentic? The most fundamental requirement is that the participants talk to one another. They must listen to the person speaking, understand what is being said, and react to it.

There is a further criterion, however, for authentic argument. Like the arguments they will engage in over the course of their adult lives, students' arguments must have a purpose and a goal. There must be a reason for having them. As Bereiter (2002) has put it:

> If an educational goal is to equip students for thinking in adult life, then discourse in school ought progressively to approximate the discourse adults engage in when they are seriously trying to understand something, to reach a decision, to solve a problem, or to produce a design (p. 361).

When these conditions are met, argument, like inquiry, becomes education for life.

If argument is not authentic—if participants do not speak to one another and the conversation has no real purpose—none of this can happen. The discourse never becomes alive. Students are left engaging in the form—taking turns speaking—minus the substance and meaning. Students may ask themselves, "Where is this conversation going, why are we having it?" They soon find the answer and do not need to keep asking the question: "This is what school is like; this is what we do here. These are things we're supposed to be learning." But whatever those things are, they likely have little to do with the skills students will draw on as adults when they are arguing about things that matter to them.

Putting Tolerance in Its Place

Simon (2001) points out that a particular mode of discourse prevails in classroom discussions, one that contrasts sharply with the discourse mode that characterizes classroom life otherwise. In most schoolwork, facts prevail and opinions are treated as an inappropriate distraction. When the time for discussion arises, both students and teacher switch gears. Opinions dominate and facts become less appropriate. Students are encouraged to voice their own opinions, and they quickly come to understand that everyone's opinion must be accorded equal respect. As a result, they are likely to feel comfortable in adding their own views to what has already been said. They are less likely, however, to feel comfortable in suggesting that someone else's view may be incorrect.

What Simon does not note is that this reverence accorded to personal opinion has specific cognitive underpinnings. Developing an understanding of the nature of knowledge and knowing (epistemological understanding) proceeds from an *absolutist* form characteristic of childhood to a *multiplist* form common by adolescence (see Chapter 2). The transition is a dramatic one: Children tend to regard knowledge as entirely factual while adolescents regard it as consisting of nothing but opinions, chosen by their owners like personal possessions and not open to challenge. No one's opinion merits being treated as better than another person's. This lack of discriminability is equated with tolerance: Because everyone has a right to their opinion, all opinions are equally right. Many adults remain multiplists for life, never progressing to the evaluativist level of epistemological understanding in which it is recognized that some opinions are in fact better than others and knowledge is understood to consist of judgments requiring support in a framework of alternatives, evidence, and argument.

Multiplist thinking conveniently reinforces certain of the values that prevail in democratic societies, notably that beliefs are a person's birthright, along with the other basic freedoms to choose where to go, what to do, and whom to associate with. Beliefs deserve respect and tolerance. And tolerance, it would seem, can only be a good thing.

Yet there is in fact a downside to tolerance. When tolerance is equated with equal merit of all claims, the ability and disposition to make discriminations—to be judgmental—is undermined. If any claim is as valid as any other, there is little reason to expend the mental effort that judging another's claims entails. Better to respect his right to have it and keep a respectful distance. Nor is there any reason to justify one's own views—it is enough simply to hold them. And we are certainly under no obligation to modify our views in response to another's arguments, unless it suits us to do so.

Tolerance, then, can translate into a willingness to listen to another's view but not to engage it. Once respective views are articulated, the inclination is to end conversation with the conclusion, "Well, I guess we disagree—to each his own." The disinclination to continue is partly one of being reluctant to invest the intellectual energy that discourse requires. But equally it is one of fearing that to criticize another's view is disrespectful, hostile, and ultimately injurious. The argument and the person are not distinguished, leaving injury to one tantamount to injury to the other. So, better to let things be, "to live and let live." To avoid the risk of being judgmental, it is safest not to judge at all. If people are going to discuss sensitive topics, indeed any topics at all, they feel they're best off doing so with people like themselves with whom they agree (an inclination that, paradoxically, leads in a direction the opposite of tolerance).

Students' ideas *about* argument—their beliefs about where, with whom, and why it might be appropriate or worthwhile—are thus as important as the skills that enable them to engage in it. As educators, we must attend to both. How do we help young people to understand the value of argument? To recognize that respect for individuals is not incompatible with serious debate of the ideas these individuals may hold?

These are difficult questions that lack pat answers. A multiplist epistemology requires significantly less intellectual energy to maintain than any other. It is not surprising that many adults never develop beyond it. Nonetheless, I offer the same general proposal with respect to argument that I do for inquiry. We must use a "boot-strapping" approach in which we engage students in the relevant activities, well before they have a firm command of the skills. With sufficient sustained exercise, they are likely to develop the skills and come to appreciate the beliefs and values on which they rest. There is one other piece, however, that needs to be part of the effort. We must model the skills and values we want young people to develop.

Modeling Skills and Values

Modern American culture is not one that holds intellectual values in high esteem. The implicit message underlying the constant reports of pollsters on every conceivable topic is that we are much more interested in *what* people think than *why*. The message is not lost on adolescents, who are much more likely to be asked to express their opinions than to support them. To *have* an opinion is all that is necessary, and the stronger the better—no teen wants to be seen as straddling a fence. It is easy to see thinking, much less arguing, as beside the point.

Education is the primary social institution that can function as a force against this cultural tide. Yet educators must recognize the importance of parents and other adults as role models of the practices and values we want adolescents' education to promote (Gardner, 1999). Botstein (1997) notes that parents all claim to want better schools for their children, but they themselves often do not live lives that demonstrate a respect for education and knowledge. In the end, we can only promote the development of intellectual values in young people to the extent that the communities of which they are a part themselves reflect these values.

The most consequential adult behaviors are those displayed toward adolescents themselves. We cannot expect adolescents to develop the disposition to engage intellectually unless we show consistency in treating adolescents as people from whom we expect serious and responsible collective and individual thought. Moshman (1993) describes two U.S. Supreme Court decisions made about the same time. One sided with high-school students who had been denied permission by their school to form a Bible study group, ruling that a school allowing extracurricular groups to meet on its premises must extend this privilege to any such group. In another ruling, however, the court upheld a high-school principal's right to censor articles written by students for the school newspaper if the principal regarded the article as "unsuitable for immature audiences." Such conflicting views regarding the intellectual competencies of adolescents are not lost on teens themselves.

My claim in this chapter has been that it is well worth the effort and challenge to identify argument as an educational goal and to press for the conditions necessary to realize it. Together with inquiry, it constitutes the best possible education we can offer young people for life. If students engage frequently in authentic argumentive discourse, they will come to understand its power as a model of knowing and its value to them in their current and future lives, and they will eventually interiorize the structure of argument as a framework for much of their own individual thinking. They will think in terms of issues and claims, with facts summoned in their service, rather than the reverse (Simon, 2001). Achieving these goals entails the development of epistemological understanding and intellectual values, as well as the development of cognitive skills.

In the next chapter, I turn to the roadmap of skills that it is necessary to attend to if these goals are to be taken seriously. In short, what needs to develop?

We begin an examination of argument skills not with the authentic dialogic arguments that we advocated in the preceding chapter as a context in which to develop argument skills, but rather with a more typical instrument that assesses students' argumentive reasoning skills. We will then proceed to make the case that the skills developed in dialogic argument lie at the heart of students' performance on such tasks.

The particular task we examine is of significant interest in its own right, due to the critical role it plays in the lives of large numbers of students. The City University of New York (CUNY) is one of a number of institutions that requires students to demonstrate skill in a test that requires argumentive reasoning. In the CUNY system, students commonly progress from one of a number of public community colleges to one of the four-year colleges of CUNY. In order to make this transition, community college students must pass a test administered by CUNY as a requirement for admission. Many students fail the test on their initial attempt and retake it a number of times. Significant percentages at each of the community colleges never pass it and are unable to continue toward a college degree in the CUNY system. At least one body of influential, policy-setting educators, then, regard the skills assessed in this test as an objective of higher education and essential to its pursuit at the degree level. Yet no coursework in the lower-level college curriculum is explicitly addressed to these skills. Let us take a look, then, at what a student is asked to do on such a test.

Coordinating Claims and Evidence in Argument

The CUNY assessment is a one-hour written examination in which the student is presented a short text, accompanied by two graphs of quantitative data, and asked to write a short essay based on this information. The graphs display some data that support the text's main claim, some that contradict it, and some that have no bearing on it. Instructions are to "state the major claims made in the reading selection and explain how data in the two graphs appear to support and/or contradict those claims." The major claim made in the text, which appears below, is that public disposal of used paper is a problem that needs to be addressed. The first of the accompanying graphs depicts the percentages of different kinds of materials—aluminum cans, yard waste, paper, steel cans, plastic bottles, and glass containers—that were recycled in 1990, in 1995, and in 2000. The second graph shows use, in tons, of office paper and of newspaper for years 1980 through 2000. Initially, newspaper use exceeds office paper use; but by 2000, paper and newspaper have reversed positions.

The following editorial recently appeared in a United States newspaper.

Ask most people what kinds of trash are clogging United States landfills, and you're likely to hear: "Beer cans, disposable diapers, glass bottles, Styrofoam cups, and packaging." Such beliefs are pure illusion. In reality, the "invisible menace" luring inside United States landfills is paper. Newspapers are especially threatening to the health of landfills, since, contrary to popular opinion, they do not biodegrade significantly. Some, unearthed after forty years of burial, have emerged relatively unscathed and completely legible.

Aggressive recycling is needed in order to reduce these mountains of paper trash, but recycling alone is not the answer. Even though Americans have steadily increased their efforts to recycle household products, recycling has not kept up with the boom in paper use fueled by the increased availability of high-speed printing and communication technologies coupled with a drop in the cost of paper. Because paper is cheap, most Americans just throw away their old newspapers, computer printouts and other paper products. Something must be done because it is clear that, as a nation, we can no longer afford to ignore the skyrocketing use of paper.

Note that students cannot perform poorly on this test because they lack a sufficient knowledge base regarding the topic. A student needs only to assemble the argument, drawing on the material made available. By doing so successfully, a student demonstrates his or her knowledge of the nature of an effective argument. In this respect, then, the test would appear to offer an ideal assessment of the understanding of argument itself.

Why do so many college-level students find the task difficult? The need to coordinate a claim and evidence bearing on it resembles the task of coordinating claim and evidence that we examined in Chapters 4 and 5 in the context of inquiry learning. In both cases, the student must identify a claim (or question, in the case of inquiry) and then identify and evaluate evidence that bears on it. In the present context, however, there exists an added complication. The claim (or question) is not necessarily one's own. Students must contemplate the writer's claim as it stands, independent of their own knowledge and ideas about its content. Why is the writer writing? What point does he or she intend to make? And what does the writer claim to know? The writer's knowledge may differ significantly from what students believe they know. Yet it is the writer's claims that require coordination with the data. Hence, a student must identify the writer's claims and represent them separately from his or her own knowledge and thinking about the topic.

I examined a sample of the test performances from a community college at which more than half of the students initially fail the CUNY test. Some students exhibited basic processing difficulties in extracting meaning from the text or interpreting the graphs. Many more, however, had problems in undertaking the next step—drawing on the data to construct a set of arguments for or against the claims made in the text. These students almost certainly would have had an easier time if they had been asked to express their own arguments for or against the claim, but that was not the assignment. They were asked to explain how data in the graphs supported the claim(s) made by the author of the text. Doing so required that they represent the claim, represent the data, and then coordinate the two.

Quite a few students, including some who neglected to identify any claim on which the data might bear, were meticulous in reading data from the graphs and recording that information in their essays. One student carefully noted, for example:

In 1990, 48% of newspaper was recycled, which increased to 55% in 1995. But unfortunately in 2000, it decreased to 53%.

Like many others, the student failed to use the information in any way or draw inferences from it. In particular, he did not relate the recycling facts from the graph to the author's claims. Other students, in addition to citing data, identified the claim they thought was being made in the text and thus did represent both the claim and the data. However, they simply juxtaposed the two, without attempting any coordination.

Among students who characterized both the data and the claim and attempted a coordination, two problems were common. Both can be characterized as failures in differentiation. First, students failed to maintain the differentiation between data and claim, instead combining the two into a single representation of "the way it is." Hence, they never recognized the possibility that the data might not be entirely consistent with the claim and might, in whole or in part, contradict it.

Second, some students did not differentiate the writer's claim from what they themselves knew or thought about the topic. As a result, the task was reduced to one that the students found easier—making their own argument for the claim. If the first differentiation failure—between data and claim— was also present, students were likely to draw selectively on the data, even distorting it as necessary, to make the best case they could for the claim. Here is an example:

> It states the devastating use of paper. Paper has been the most useful prod-uct in the century and is also the cheapest . . . People use paper for many things, but later they don't know what to do with it. An example is outside in the streets they give you paper with announcements, you read it and then throw it away. That's why our streets are full of garbage and mostly of paper . . . The charts state very clearly the same as the lecture; that paper is the most product use because it is cheaper.

In some cases, the distinction between claim and data was lost. In the next example, the claim was presented as deriving directly from the data:

> Graph 2 shows how recycling newspaper has decreased a lot. Furthermore, it shows us the importance of recycle[ing] newspaper, plastic, glass, etc.

Although graph 2, in fact, shows paper use, not recycling, what is notable is the student's characterization of the claim as embedded in the evidence, rather than the evidence as distinct from the claim and bearing on it.

In the following case, the student endeavored to make use of the data; but in so doing, the writer's purpose and perspective were sacrificed entirely:

> We cannot ignore aluminum cans as also being a menace.

Even students who represented both data and claim more or less accu-rately and sought to connect them sometimes went astray because they did not take the writer's statements as assertions to be evaluated in the light of independent empirical evidence. This student, for example, attempted a so-phisticated linkage of claim and data:

> Since newspapers are the lowest in the year 2000, and [the writer] clearly states that newspapers are the most harmful, maybe we have already started to do something to help alleviate our landfill problems.

This student apparently never considered that the data she cited could be evidence against the writer's claim.

A major stumbling block, it appears, is students' failure to distinguish their own perspective from that of the writer making the claims. The student, in other words, becomes one with the writer. Such an identity fusion could possibly help a student to understand and appreciate the writer's perspective. Instead, however, it appeared to have the unproductive consequence of permanently collapsing the writer's and the student's vantage points into one. Students were not able to step into the writer's shoes temporarily and then step back and resume their own perspective. Hence, everything that students knew or inferred was attributed to the writer. The knowledge could then be drawn on to make their (and the writer's) claim convincing.

In so doing, students lost the opportunity to treat the writer's text as an object of cognition—to step back from it, look at it (rather than enter into it), and reason *about* it. As a result, they could not construct relations between the text and evidence that might bear upon it. Chapters 4 and 5 addressed the need for students to ask, "*What* do I know?" and "*How* do I know?" Students must also learn to ask, "What, and how, does the writer know?" while preserving the distinction between their own and the writer's perspectives and knowledge. In addition, they must accurately represent available data, distinct from the writer's claims and from their own knowledge.

If this is done correctly, the result is a triangle that allows the student to construct relationships between any two of its three points, defined by self's perspective, other's perspective, and evidence (Figure 7.1). If the student is unable to construct and maintain representations of each of the three points of the triangle, it becomes impossible to construct relations among them. As a worst case, the three points collapse into a single representation of "what is," which then becomes the student's only basis for making an argument of any sort.

Examining and making judgments about relationships among claims and evidence are higher-order cognitive skills that develop only with practice. Chapter 5 examines methods for scaffolding their development when such skills are too weakly developed to function autonomously. In the present case, one way to ease students' cognitive load might be to provide a clearly identified claim and supporting argument and ask students to judge it. Students are relieved of the task of having to draw on a larger body of material to construct arguments themselves; yet in judging ready-made arguments, they might still exhibit understanding of what constitutes an effective argu-

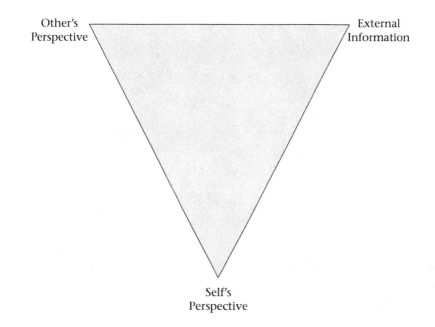

Other's
Perspective

External
Information

Self's
Perspective

Figure 7.1. Coordination of three perspectives required in argument evaluation.

ment. Do students do any better under these conditions? This is the question I turn to next.

Evaluating Arguments

Kuhn and Felton (2000) examined the argumentive reasoning of eighth graders (from a school in the same neighborhood as and very similar to the struggling school), urban college students (from the same community college described earlier in this chapter), and masters-level graduate students in education. Students were presented two arguments in support of a claim and asked to choose which was the stronger and to justify why. One argument offered a theoretical explanation of mechanism that made the claim plausible, whereas the other offered empirical evidence that the claim was true. (See Box 7.1.) More important than students' choices were the reasons given to justify them. In addition to selecting the stronger argument, students were asked to indicate the strengths and weaknesses (if any) of that argument as well as the strengths (if any) and weaknesses of the other argument.

Box 7.1

ARGUMENT EVALUATION

Pick the better argument, A or B, for the question, "Why do teenagers start smoking?"

A. Smith says it is because they see ads that make smoking look attractive. A good-looking guy in neat clothes with a cigarette in his mouth is someone you would like to be like.
B. Jones says it is because they see ads that make smoking look attractive. When cigarette ads were banned from TV, smoking went down.

Pick the better argument, A or B, for the question "Do vitamins protect people from getting sick?"

A. Ed says they do. The people in his office who take vitamins are absent from work much less than the people who do not take vitamins.
B. Bill says they do. The vitamins strengthen the body's fighting power and make it better able to fight off illnesses.

Although, as one would expect, the graduate students did best and the college students did better than the eighth graders, only a minority of students exhibited understanding of the epistemic strengths and weaknesses of the two argument types (evidence-based and explanation-based) depicted in Table 7.1. Epistemic characteristics of an argument pertain to its form rather than to its content. Epistemic characteristics apply to any argument of a given general form; nonepistemic characteristics apply only to the argument's particular content. Appreciating the epistemic characteristics of an argument thus reflects understanding of the structure of argument itself.

Students' nonepistemic judgments regarding the arguments typically addressed the claim's correctness (for example, "This is a good argument because it's true; those ads do make kids want to smoke") rather than the quality of the argument supporting the claim. The percentages of students citing epistemic strengths of explanation-based argument (for example, "It gives a reason") ranged from 30 percent among the eighth graders to 60 percent among the graduate students. The percentages citing the epistemic strengths of evidence-based argument (for example, "It really happened") ranged from 11 percent to 76 percent across age groups. Percentages citing the epistemic weakness of explanation (for example, "It could be wrong") were lower, ranging from 0 percent to 26 percent, and the fewest students— 2 percent to 10 percent—cited the epistemic weakness of evidence (for ex-

Table 7.1. Types of student responses regarding the strengths and weaknesses of two argument types

Epistemic judgments	Nonepistemic judgments
Strengths of explanation-based argument	
It explains why	It makes sense
It gives a reason	It seems more reasonable
It gives a theory	It's my own experience
It illustrates	It's common knowledge
It's more scientific	It's true
It says more things	It's a proven fact
Strengths of evidence-based argument	
It provides empirical evidence	It sounds better
It gives facts	It gives an example
It shows proof	It gives more detail
It really happened	It's right, because TV is powerful
It's objective rather than subjective	
Weaknesses of explanation-based argument	
It may or may not be true	Vitamins may have no effect
It's merely an opinion	Not everyone can take vitamins
It could be wrong	Cigarette ads are not just shown on TV
It's just a theory	
It doesn't have any support	
Weaknesses of evidence-based argument	
It's only a statistical, indirect reason, not a scientific reason	Some people can't take vitamins
It doesn't say why	

ample, "It doesn't say why"). (See Table 7.1 for other examples of each type of response.)

The difficulties students exhibited in this task were similar to those they showed in the task examined in the preceding section. Their own perspective dominated, and the perspective of the individual making the argument was subsumed to it. Hence they expressed their own evaluation of the claim itself rather than undertaking what the task required—evaluating the *relationship* between a claim made by another person and the support that person has offered for it. In this way, students reduced the algorithm for evaluating an argument to a very simple one: If I favor the claim, an argument supporting it is a good argument; if I oppose the claim, an argument supporting it is a bad argument. The quality of the argument itself—its epistemic strength as an argument—does not enter into the judgment.

Under this algorithm, a good argument for a rejected claim becomes an impossibility. Yet we shall see it is exactly this combination that is both the most important and most difficult to address in a dialogic argument. You must take the perspective of the opponent, envision their claim as true, and then seek ways to weaken the argument that gives their claim its force.

Constructing Personal Arguments

Because constructing or evaluating an argument for or against someone else's claim requires identifying the other's perspective and coordinating it with the other elements in Figure 7.1, might students do better if they were relieved of this cognitive burden and asked simply to construct their own argument in support of a claim? Then they are representing solely their own perspective and seeking to advance their own agenda, not anyone else's. They are more likely to feel ownership of the arguments they make. What cognitive skills do students exhibit under these conditions?

In a series of studies (Kuhn, Shaw, and Felton, 1997; Felton and Kuhn, 2001; Kuhn and Udell, 2003), we asked students of different ages to construct arguments on the topic of capital punishment. As noted in Chapter 6, the inner-city, "disadvantaged" teens and young adults we worked with felt comfortable talking about the topic and felt entitled to have views about it, which was not true of a number of other topics we explored.

Our initial step was to ask students to indicate their opinions either in favor of or against capital punishment and then to offer an argument in support of their position. We examined these arguments on a number of dimensions; but for the moment, I focus on a primary one—the extent to which the argument that a student offered was one- or two-sided. In other words, did the arguer address the opposing view (favoring capital punishment, if the arguer was against it; or opposing capital punishment, if the arguer favored it)? Or did the arguer focus exclusively on his or her own position, making arguments in its favor, while ignoring the alternative position? A slightly different way to put the question is to ask whether the arguers situated their arguments within a framework of alternatives. If they were against capital punishment, did they make an argument not simply as to why the practice is bad but why it is worse than the alternatives that would be practiced in its place? If they were in favor, did they address why capital punishment is preferable to these alternatives?

The answer was often negative. Students varied considerably in how much they had to say in support of their position. Some offered a number of different reasons to justify their position and others only one. The common feature that a majority of their arguments shared, however, was a confinement to the merits of their own position. The opposing position—the merits of capital punishment if the arguer was opposed or its drawbacks if the arguer was in favor—was never addressed. Nor was a framework of alternatives invoked—how did the practice compare to the alternatives that would replace it? There appear below several examples. As the two-sided example makes clear, two-sided arguments are not necessarily more sophisticated than one-sided arguments. Their defining characteristic is simply that they include reasons to favor both positions.

One-sided

Teen: If someone did something wrong, they should be subject to capital punishment. (Why is that?) Because for instance if they kill someone, maybe the same thing is due to them. (Any other reason?) Well, I feel that people should pay if they did something wrong.

Adult: I believe that the government has a responsibility toward the criminal as well as the victim. The government should treat criminals as patients with emotional and mental problems and treat them for their disorder instead of ending their lives. I believe everyone should die of natural cause, and that murder is murder regardless of who performs the act. Capital punishment is simply murder.

Two-sided

Adult: I have mixed feelings about capital punishment because if it were my family and they did something bad I wouldn't want them to be put to death. [But] if it was someone I loved [that was murdered] and they died, I would want the person to die.

About the same proportion of young teens (seventh and eighth graders) and young adults (community college students) expressed two-sided arguments—31 percent of teens and 34 percent of adults (based on group sizes of forty nine and forty four, respectively); the remainder's arguments were confined to reasons supporting one position (Kuhn et al., 1997). Adults, however, were somewhat more likely to present their arguments in a framework of alternatives. For example, they argued that life imprisonment is a better alternative than capital punishment or that life imprisonment is not a viable alternative and capital punishment is therefore necessary. Only 6 percent (three students) of the teens, versus 23 percent of the adults, offered such arguments (Kuhn et al., 1997).

Co-Constructing Dialogic Arguments

If students' skills are weak in constructing their own arguments, what can we expect when they engage in the seemingly more challenging task of dialogic argument with an opponent? Chapter 6 raises the possibility that the dialogic context may, in fact, be an easier one for novice arguers. It is a form they are familiar with from everyday experience, and the "missing other" does not have to be invoked in imaginary form in order to address his or her arguments. The opponent is right there, playing this role him- or herself. The novice arguer need only play his or her own role in such a dialog, and familiar conversational norms provide a scaffold for the exchange.

How, then, do students fare when asked to engage in a dialogic argument with a peer who holds an opposing view? We investigated this question by asking students from the same middle-school and community college populations described earlier to engage in a discussion of the merits of capital punishment with a peer whose view opposed theirs (Felton and Kuhn, 2001; Kuhn et al., 1997; Kuhn and Udell, 2003). The pair was asked to talk for about ten minutes and to try to come to agreement if they could.

Students were amenable and appeared to enjoy the activity. Yet, the dialogic context did not have as great a benefit as it might have. Some pairs did little more than express their respective views and leave them there, juxtaposed with one another, with neither member of the pair attempting to engage, or even express a reaction to, the arguments of the other. The object of the encounter in their eyes, it appeared, was to let their views be aired and, once that objective was met, they perceived the task as completed. In some pairs, one member played the role of interlocutor for the other, helping the partner to articulate a viewpoint by means of probing questions. Occasionally, the two switched roles. But neither partner questioned or commented on the other's argument.

Some excerpts from the young teens' dialogic arguments appear in Box 7.2. The first, between T and C, illustrates the simple airing of respective positions, without engagement. In the second, between A and L, A assumes the interlocutor role, even probing L's position by posing limiting conditions ("But what about if it's serious?"). A then tries to switch roles, by introducing a statement of her own position, but L is unable to assume the interlocutor role and instead further elaborates her own view.

The two final examples in Box 7.2 reflect greater skill. The partners begin to engage one another's positions. They do so only in the most elementary way, however. Rather than mutually exploring the reasoning underlying one another's positions, they seek some practical solution that would be ac-

BOX 7.2

EXAMPLES OF YOUNG ADOLESCENTS' DYADIC ARGUMENTS ON CAPITAL PUNISHMENT

Example 1: T and C

T: Well I think capital punishment is a good idea because if somebody does a crime, I think they should be put to death for it.

C: I think that people shouldn't be put to death for whatever they do because two wrongs don't make a right.

T: Yeah, well, I think the person that got killed, their family would want that murderer to die too.

C: I don't think people should be put to death. I think the other way. I don't think people should be put to death. Like I said, two wrongs don't make a right. They have to pay for their consequences, which is to be put in jail.

T: She ain't going to change her mind, so . . . [dialog ends]

Example 2: A and L

A: Are you for capital punishment?

L: No.

A: You are against it?

L: Somewhat.

A: Why?

L: Because I don't think people should die for stupid things.

A: Yeah. But what about if it's serious?

L: Oh, then they should die.

A: What? So are you against it?

L: Somewhat. But I'm not sure.

A: I'm for it. But my opinion could change.

L: Yep.

A: Because I feel if you do something wrong, you should be able to pay for it.

L: If I did something wrong, I think I should die.

Example 3: M and J

M: I am for capital punishment because I think if somebody does a bad crime or kills somebody that they should have to have capital punishment because they should not be killing people and just not be punished.

J: I am against capital punishment because I feel that if a person does a crime they should suffer. They shouldn't get it over and just be killed. I feel they should go to jail and have to deal with people raping them and stuff like that because they deserve it.

M: A little bit I'm for it because I think that if it's somebody like if you look at it from if the person is in your family and you don't want them to get killed and they should just go to jail because that's enough punishment if they get it for a long time.

J: I mean if they're in jail, your family members could still see you or whatever.

M: Yeah.

Example 4: E and M

E: I have mixed feelings on capital punishment . . . If you know what you did and you did it, you should be executed for it. But if you did it because you were like emotionally upset about it, you don't deserve to die . . . It's all about the physical and mental state that you was in to do the crime.

M: I think that you should have to face capital punishment if you kill somebody because you shouldn't kill nobody. But on the other side I think that some people don't agree with it because they think that if it was their family, they wouldn't want nobody to get killed.

E: But suppose you didn't kill somebody intentionally. You didn't do it on purpose. You didn't do it because you just felt like, "Oh, maybe that person should die." You did it because you were emotionally upset.

M: I don't think that nobody should like not think they should get capital punishment just because they didn't do it on purpose. It's a fact that somebody's family is not with them no more. So I think they should still have to get capital punishment because somebody's family member is missing.

E: I don't think that's fair because if somebody in your family killed somebody because you were hurt or deceased or you were in the hospital in intensive care, they shouldn't have to get a lethal injection . . . But if they killed that person for no reason because they were looking at you wrong or something like that, yes they do deserve to die.

M: Then, alright, I feel they are going to have a long time in jail. Because they killed somebody, [even] if they don't think that they did it on purpose.

E: Alright, you are right. They should sit in jail and suffer and think about what they did. And think about maybe there could have been another way to solve what I did, to redo it.

M: If it's not on purpose, you should just go to jail.

ceptable to them both. Finding such a solution, in their view, would complete their task. M and J, for example, begin with opposing positions and end up agreeing on a long jail term as an alternative to capital punishment. Their reasons for accepting this alternative, however, have little in common. J accepts it because she sees it as inflicting appropriate suffering to punish the misdeed, while M's reasoning focuses on the feelings of family members.

In the final example in Box 7.2, E and M show the greatest dialogic skill. They converse at length (only excerpts appear in the box), honing in on points of difference in their positions. At least at some points, they address one another's arguments, although, like many pairs, their discussion is limited to the less-advanced arguments highlighting the conditions under which capital punishment is appropriate; they do not cover arguments concerning the functions or purposes of capital punishment (see Chapter 8 for more detail on argument types). Nevertheless, like M and J, they are satisfied with identifying a practical solution acceptable to them both as fulfillment of their task. This objective, as it was for M and J, can be fulfilled without appealing to arguments at all.

Negotiating the Demands of Discourse

Older students more frequently, although not always, produce dialogs that are attuned to the demands of discourse (Felton and Kuhn, 2001). Here I focus attention on less skilled students, to better understand the cognitive demands that discourse poses.

Why do students exhibit difficulties in engaging in genuine argumentive discourse on a topic they have ideas about and are comfortable with? Do they not understand the objectives of such discourse? Or do they lack the cognitive skills that it requires?

One way to characterize the weaknesses students display in dialogic argument is to say that they do not know how to talk to one another, at least in this context. (In contexts outside of school, we know that they converse, and disagree, with ease.) This interpretation is consistent, certainly, with what we observed in classroom activities intended to involve dialogic argument (see Chapter 6). Perhaps, however, the requirements of the classroom debate activities were not clear to students. They might not have understood what they were supposed to do. In the activity described here, the social context was more structured and greatly simplified. A student interacted with one peer whose position on a topic had been established, and the pair was given clear instructions regarding their task.

Despite this more structured context, many students largely failed to engage one another's claims. The cognitive resources of the least skilled pairs appeared to be consumed with the tasks of constructing and expressing justifications for the position to which they had publicly committed themselves. Only infrequently did they attempt the genuine exchange that is the mark of authentic discourse. Why? Attention to their peer's ideas might have created cognitive overload. Or considering these ideas might simply not have been recognized as part of the task. Most likely, both factors were at work—both procedural and meta-level limitations constrained performance.

As a result, the task of dialogic argument is reduced to one curiously like that of individual argument. The objective is the same in both cases—to make the most compelling case possible as to the merits of the chosen position. Arguers say to themselves, "If I do a good enough job, my position will prevail, outshining any competitors, which will fade away without further consideration." In the case of individual argument, the task is taken on as a solitary endeavor. In the case of dialogic argument, the task is similarly individual but two people engage in it simultaneously, juxtaposing their respective efforts in a respectful turn-taking format. They act jointly without genuinely engaging one another, or at most engage in a superficial way.

Many, and perhaps most, argumentive dialogs occupy some intermediate position between this kind of pseudo-argument and highly skilled dialogic argument. The latter requires coordination of the dual goals of dialogic argument: to secure commitments from the opponent that can be used to support one's own claims and to undermine the opponent's position by identifying and challenging unwarranted claims (Walton, 1989). Both of these require attention to the opponent's assertions and the endeavor to influence them.

Each of the utterances in a dialogic argument can be classified according to whether its function is to advance the speaker's claims or to address the claims of the opponent. In analyses of students' dialogic arguments, we have assessed the proportion of each partner's utterances that were addressed to the other's claims versus ones that were focused on exposition of a student's own claims and arguments. The most powerful way to address an opponent's claim, given the goals of dialogic argument, is to advance a counterargument that removes or reduces the force of the claim. The opponent, of course, can come back with a counterargument of his or her own—a rebuttal—with the goal of restoring the force of the original claim. A weaker form of counterargument we observed in students' dialogs was the expression of an alternative to the opponent's argument. A counterargu-

ment of this type does not directly address the weaknesses of the opponent's argument; instead, the alternative is implied to be more worthy. The
weakest form of counterargument (arguably not qualifying as a counterargument at all) is simple disagreement with an opponent's argument, in
the absence of any reasons or alternatives. Such disagreement nonetheless
does at least reflect attention to the opponent's view.

We compared the total percentage of these other-focused utterances in
students' argumentive dialogs to the percentage of utterances that were self-
focused, consisting of elaborations or clarifications of the student's own
claims (Felton and Kuhn, 2001). Among young teens, an average of 11 percent of utterances consisted of one or another form of these other-focused
utterances. Among community college adults, this percentage increased to
24 percent. Conversely, the average percentage of teens' utterances devoted
to exposition of their own position was 43 percent, compared to 36 percent
among adults. Differences between the two groups were not huge, but large
enough to suggest developing argument skills in the years from early adolescence to early adulthood, even within populations who are not highly accomplished academically. Interestingly, adolescents (but not adults) used
the various kinds of counterarguments equally often when they were asked
to engage in dialogs with peers holding agreeing positions as they did in
dialogs with disagreeing peers (Felton and Kuhn, 2001). Counterargument,
then, appears not to serve the same function in their discourse as it does in
the discourse of more skilled adult arguers.

Learning to Argue

Dialogic argument, it appears, despite its roots in everyday conversation, is
not an intuitively given skill. Like inquiry, it is tempting to see argument as
a human competence at the disposition of the untutored child, executed
spontaneously and effortlessly, with the educator's only challenge to make
sure that the skill is kept alive and vigorous. Like the disposition to investigate the world, a young child's disposition to make claims and enter them
into a social arena needs to be developed into a set of crucially important
skills. These are skills that by no means "come naturally": They develop
only as the product of sustained engagement, practice, and investment of
cognitive effort.

In this chapter I have identified some rudimentary cognitive skills entailed in authentic argument. They include understanding the objectives of
argument: engaging the other's claims with the goal of weakening them,
while advancing arguments that strengthen one's own position. Meeting

these dual objectives requires coordination of particular argument strategies (such as exposition and counterargument) with objectives, coordination of objectives with one another, and coordination of the multiple perspectives that exist in any argument. Evaluating arguments poses the further challenge of judging how well others have fulfilled these goals.

I began this chapter by looking at a test of argumentive thinking that is employed as a "high-stakes" admission gate to a college degree. Few would probably quarrel with the assertion that students aspiring to a college degree should be able to meet the challenges this test poses. Yet a significant number of students seeking a higher degree fail the test, at some institutions at a rate exceeding 50 percent. Should these students take their failure as proof that they are not suited for higher education? Many no doubt have. But at least a few have reacted with dismay and questioned the message. "Which courses are these skills taught in?" they want to know. "Why haven't we learned them? What can I do now to learn what I need to?" These students have a legitimate complaint, certainly. If these skills are so highly valued, why are courses not available that teach them?

English instructors, and even instructors in other fields, may counter that expository writing skills are a major focus of their instruction. Yet expressing ideas clearly in writing is not the same thing as negotiating the cognitive demands of effective argument. Moreover, constructing individual arguments, especially in writing, may not be the most effective way to build argument skills. Students often do not understand the purpose of their writing, beyond fulfilling a course requirement (Graff, 2003). They lack the "missing other" with whom they are disagreeing, the individual in contrast to whom they can articulate their own position.

It is in dialogic argument, I propose, that students can discover this purpose and best develop the foundation of skills that will serve them in a variety of other, including more traditionally academic, contexts. The next chapter explores this possibility further.

In this chapter we pursue the idea that dialogic argument provides the most productive context in which to develop argument skills. Dialogic argument builds on the familiar activity of everyday conversation in a way that an academic writing assignment or even a verbal argument supporting a claim does not. The format is well known and practiced in everyday life. I attend to what you are saying to me, and I endeavor to make meaning from it. While awaiting a cue that you have finished speaking, I begin to formulate a response that addresses what you have said. I expect that once I begin speaking, you will do the same. In this way, two people's actions relate to one another, with each person's actions shaping those of the other in a way that does not occur in many other contexts—for example, when two students respond successively to a teacher's question.

A Reason to Argue

If as educators we ask two students to engage in a serious discussion, we build on this foundation of everyday conversation. Young adolescents show at least some degree of skill in engaging in such discussions. They are able to express their respective views and acknowledge their disagreements. One partner, we saw (see Chapter 7) may even scaffold the other's articulation of a position by posing probing questions. But going further, to jointly construct a productive dialogic argument, requires more skill and understanding than the practice of everyday conversation provides by this age.

Participants in dialogic argument certainly need cognitive skills—to judge possibilities and select the most effective response once they have digested their partner's contribution, and then to do so again and again for as long as the dialog lasts. This process is cognitively demanding, to say the least. And so if they are to be disposed to invest the considerable effort that is required, participants in a dialogic argument need to have formed some understanding of its purpose. They need at least a provisional answer to the questions:

Why argue? What is the point? What are we trying to accomplish? Can we hope to construct an argument that will be more than the juxtaposition of our two positions? What will we take away from the effort? Can we hope to achieve anything more than agreeing to disagree?

Answers to these questions rest on the development of the epistemological understanding that Chapter 2 examines. If all truths are out in the world awaiting discovery, as the absolutist sees it, or if there is no truth beyond individual predilection, as the multiplist maintains, there is indeed no point to argument. It does not pay to invest the cognitive effort required. As educators, we can ask such students to partake in dialogic argument and they will oblige. But they will be doing little more than going through a routine whose purpose they do not appreciate.

Although many middle-school and high-school teachers say they provide frequent opportunities for student debate, authentic dialogic argument is indeed difficult to achieve in classrooms—in disadvantaged schools like the struggling school, in advantaged schools like the best-practice school, and most likely in the vast majority of schools that lie between these extremes. Ms. B at the struggling school had students prepare by writing essays listing reasons for their positions, which they then presented in the debate. Mrs. O at the best-practice school encouraged a less explicit but similar form of preparation. The outcome was largely the same, despite the many striking differences in the abilities and experiences of the two groups of students. Students in both classrooms rarely spoke directly *to* one another as they presented their prepared material. A student's speech was rarely influenced by what the previous speaker had said.

Neither the form of the discussion in these classrooms, then, nor the topic drew on the resemblance between argumentive discourse and everyday conversation. Students in both classrooms appeared to accept the activity as one of the many expected of them as part of their school life. At the best-practice school, students understood the primary purpose of the activity as helping them to acquire and retain the information on which they would soon be tested. Students at the struggling school had long ceased asking themselves what the purpose was of any of the things they were required to do at school and they simply drew what enjoyment they could from the activity.

Getting into Arguments

How, then, do we help students to develop the skills of argument if they have yet to acquire its epistemological underpinnings? The challenge is more formidable than the parallel one we encounter with inquiry skills. "Finding out" has intuitive appeal that is not quite so dependent on a student's level of epistemological understanding. It is harder to see a reason to argue, especially because the alternatives of "agreeing to disagree" and "live and let live" are held in such high esteem in our culture.

This chapter examines an extended activity designed to develop the argument skills of students who do not yet see the value of argument. In a word, the rationale is to engage them in dense practice of argument, allowing them to see its benefits at the same time as they exercise and gradually develop the skills needed to execute it well. Microgenetic research (Kuhn, 1995; Siegler, 2006) provides a basis for anticipating success. Many kinds of cognitive skills have been shown to improve (in both quality and frequency of use) as a result of frequent engagement with problems that require their use.

Participants in the program I describe in this chapter were at-risk, low-achieving students from the struggling school, several middle schools in the same urban neighborhood as the struggling school, and a group of boys aged sixteen to twenty from a residential detention center for delinquent teens. Our rationale was that these academically disadvantaged students were the ones least likely to appreciate the purpose and benefits of argumentive discourse. If we were successful in encouraging them to value argument and to develop the skills it entails, we would have reason to feel confident that the same success could be achieved at least as readily among more advantaged populations.

Initially we experimented with simple dyadic argument, drawing on the rationale of engagement and practice as mechanisms sufficient to induce development (Kuhn et al., 1997). Over a period of weeks, we asked students to engage in dialogic arguments with a series of different classmates who held an opposing (or, in some cases, an agreeing) position on capital punishment. Students were paired with a different partner on each occasion and, as Chapter 7 describes, the pair was asked to talk for about ten minutes and to try to come to agreement if they could. In the present case, however, students were asked several days later to repeat this same activity with a new partner, until they had engaged in a total of five dialogs.

Would this simple engagement in, and practice of, argumentive discourse enhance students' skills? In the initial study (Kuhn et al., 1997), we looked at effects of this experience on students' individual arguments. In a later study, conducted by Felton (2004) and focused on progress in dialogic argument, middle-school students similarly engaged in a series of dialogs over a period of weeks. This time, however, they alternated between the roles of participant and peer adviser, with the latter role intended to heighten reflective awareness of their argumentive discourse. After a dialog, the two participants met separately with their peer advisers (who had observed the dialog). Participant and adviser together reviewed the dialog (scaffolded by a checklist that encouraged them to identify what were termed "reasons," "criticism," and "defense"), examining the quality of what the participant had offered within each category, and considering what the participant might have done better and why.

Results based on this approach were encouraging. Differences in types of argument strategy used at initial and subsequent assessments were similar to the differences observed between adolescents and adults described in Chapter 7. In other words, the dialogic arguments of middle-school students became more "adult-like" in two respects. First, students decreased the percentage of talk devoted to exposition of their own views. Second, they increased the percentage of talk devoted to arguments against the other participant's position (counterargument). Because these gains transferred to the students' dialogs on a topic that had not been discussed previously, we had reason to think that they had developed argumentive discourse skills, not simply become more conversant with the topic they were discussing. Moreover, students who participated in the reflective activity with peer advisers showed greater gains than those in a comparison group who engaged only in the dialogs (Felton, 2004). And finally, participation in dialogic argumentation led to advancement in students' individual arguments as well (Kuhn et al., 1997; Felton, 2004).

Playing to Win

As promising as these results were, a critical question remained unaddressed. What had students come to understand *about* argument, as distinct from the skills they may have developed for engaging in it? What did they think they were accomplishing in these dialogs? Were they simply going along with another activity that an adult authority figure had asked them to do? We might have tried assessing their understanding of argument and its purposes before and after the experience, but we were doubtful that we would detect much change after so few opportunities to engage in the activity.

Something critical we had neglected to offer students, we concluded, was a reason to be doing what we were asking them to do—a reason that would make sense from their point of view. We needed to help them recognize a reason to argue, a reason that would keep them engaged until, we hoped, they discovered for themselves some of the deeper, more lasting benefits that argument confers.

This objective led to development of the argument curriculum described in this chapter. To maximize our chances of success, we reasoned, we needed to build that curriculum on activities and ideas familiar to the population for which it was intended—academically disadvantaged students who have not bought into scholarship as a worthwhile endeavor. While the rituals and routines of scholarship hold little appeal for these young people, they are familiar with conversation and its norms. And they exhibit mastery, even, of distinct conversational genres that adhere to diverse norms, as evidenced, for example, in conversations with their peers in contrast to conversations with adult authority figures.

These youth also are experienced in getting into arguments with their peers. Their arguments are most often brief and explosive and of more social and emotional than intellectual significance. In a word, an argument is something you try to win. You want to prevail over your adversary. We therefore began with this reality and sought to draw these nonacademically oriented students into richer, more sustained argument than they were accustomed to. Our goal was to enrich, indeed transform, their understanding of argument during a sustained period in which they were deeply involved in its practice.

Following is a summary of the activities and associated cognitive goals that constitute the argument curriculum:

Generating reasons
  Goals: Reasons underlie opinions; different reasons may underlie the same opinion
Elaborating reasons
  Goal: Good reasons support opinions.
Supporting reasons with evidence
  Goal: Evidence can strengthen reasons.
Evaluating reasons
  Goal: Some reasons are better than others.
Developing reasons into an argument
  Goal: Reasons connect to one another and are building blocks of argument.
Examining and evaluating opposing side's reasons
  Goal: Opponents have reasons too.
Generating counterarguments to others' reasons
  Goal: Opposing reasons can be countered. "We can fight this."

Generating rebuttals to others' counterarguments
Goal: Counters to reasons can be rebutted. "We have a comeback."
Contemplating mixed evidence
Goal: Evidence can be used to support different claims.
Conducting and evaluating two-sided arguments
Goal: Some arguments are stronger than others.

In the following section, I describe the activities in more details as they transpired with some variation over roughly a ten-week period in a range of different settings, from a conventional eighth-grade classroom to a residential detention facility. Students worked in small groups during one or two class periods per week. Several adults served as coaches who helped the team achieve its goals.

Getting Started

As a prelude to the program, students' skills in both individual and dialogic argument were assessed. They were first asked to generate their own arguments for or against capital punishment. They were then paired with a partner who held an opposing view and asked to engage in a discussion of the topic and to try to reach agreement.

The program itself was introduced as a special project (in either their Social Studies or English class, depending on the school) they would be working on for several months. Capital punishment was described as a topic that currently generates much public debate and impacts many people's lives. We told the students that we hoped their work would contribute to thinking about the topic.

Based on their own initial opinions, students were then formed into pro and con teams of four to eight students each. At a final "showdown," we explained, their team would be pitted against an opposing team, and one of the two teams would be declared the victor and would participate in a special event to celebrate. Their job in the next months was to prepare for the showdown.

At each of the subsequent sessions, each pro and con team met separately with an adult coach. The teams (and their respective coaches) did not interact until near the end of the activity. Teams were scheduled to meet twice a week for a ninety-minute period for a total of sixteen sessions over eight weeks. Standardized testing, school assemblies, holidays, and school vacations, however, extended the period over which the sessions took place to most of a semester, or approximately twelve weeks.

Teams progressed through the sequence of activities that constitutes the curriculum at approximately the same pace, but with latitude for the participants and coach to stay with an activity until they reached closure. On average, about 1.5 sessions were devoted to each activity (with its associated goal). In many of the activities, participants separated into two or three pairs or triads to work independently and then reassembled to discuss their work as a group.

Activity 1: Generating Reasons

Participants were asked to remember the reasons they gave in the initial interview for their opinion regarding capital punishment and to select the most important of those reasons. Large index cards were distributed and the participants wrote their most important reason on a card. The coach provided a rationale for every activity in which the team engaged; as an example, for this first activity, a coach for the pro team said, "The first step is to be clear about *why* we think capital punishment (CP) is good. We saw in talking with each of you that people can have different reasons for thinking it is good, so we need to get these reasons out on the table and decide what we think of them."

Participants were encouraged to interpret reasons ("What does this one mean?" "Is there a different way to say this?") and to eliminate duplicates. They then generated and recorded as many additional reasons as they could and the cycle of reflection and elimination of duplicates was repeated. Deciding whether reasons were duplicates of each other proved a fruitful source of deliberation regarding a reason's meaning.

As a homework assignment, students were asked to interview and bring in the reasons of three people who held the same position they did on capital punishment; at the next session, these reasons were dealt with in the same way. (The coach added at most one reason to this discussion, if she identified any major gaps in the list that the group generated.)

Activity 2: Elaborating Reasons

Participants were asked to reflect on whether their reasons were good, which led to a discussion of what makes a reason good and to revision of the wording of some of the reasons. The criterion of how a person with an opposing view would react to the reason was introduced. Possible ways to strengthen reasons were considered. The pro coach introduced the distinction between genuine *why* reasons, justifying why CP is a good idea, and *when* reasons, specifying conditions for its use. Each participant was asked to claim "ownership" of at least one reason that he or she would be responsible for from that point through the showdown.

Activity 3: Supporting Reasons with Evidence

The concept of evidence as strengthening a reason was made explicit. Students discussed types of evidence and were given several newspaper articles with stories or statistics that supported their position. Pairs read the articles together and reported to the group, and the group decided together how the information might strengthen any of their reasons. A summary of supporting evidence was noted on an "evidence card" that was physically connected to each reason card.

Activity 4: Evaluating Reasons

In pairs or triads, participants were given duplicate sets of the team's reason cards and asked to reach agreement on how to sort them into three categories ("best," "good," and "okay"). This activity was repeated with new subgroups and finally as a whole group. Reasons remained in the top category only if participants could justify (with "reasons for reasons") to the group's satisfaction why it belonged there. Individual ownership of each of the final set of top reasons was established. It was agreed that each team member would take charge of at least one of the reasons and be responsible for it.

Activity 5: Developing Reasons into an Argument

Initially in pairs and then all together, the team worked to construct and format on poster board an argument based on their set of top reasons. This activity required discussion of which reasons to use, the relationships between reasons and the possibility of connecting words or phrases, the order of presentation, and the inclusion of examples and evidence. After practice presentations, the group chose one member to present the argument, which was recorded on video for subsequent analysis and critique by the group. How the presentation could be used at the showdown was discussed.

Activity 6: Examining and Evaluating the Opposing Side's Reasons

Students were prompted to consider what the opposing team had been doing during this time and what reasons they might have generated. The coach led participants to the recognition that it would be useful to know what these reasons are ("Why would we want to know their reasons? What will we want to do with them?"). The coach then disclosed that she had reached an agreement with the coach of the opposing team to exchange reasons. She provided the set of the opposing team's reasons to the group. After some animated discussion of the wisdom of this exchange, attention turned to examination of the cards. Participants were divided into subgroups to evaluate the opposing side's reasons by sorting them into strong, middle, and weak categories, as they had done with their own reasons.

Activity 7: Generating Counterarguments to Others' Reasons

The generation of counterarguments, which began spontaneously in the preceding activity, was formalized. Participants were divided into pairs and given colored "counter" cards on which to record counterarguments to each other-side reason. Pairs were reformed and the group then reassembled to select the strongest counter to each other-side reason. When agreement was reached, that counter was attached to the reason card and one member of the team took ownership of it.

Activity 8: Generating Rebuttals to Others' Counterarguments

The team's own reason cards were returned to them, with counterargument cards produced by the opposing team attached. In pairs, team members debated how to respond—whether they should strengthen their reason to avoid the criticism, rebut the criticism, or drop the reason. Where appropriate, rebuttals were generated. The goal of reducing the strength of the counterargument was developed and agreed on. After different pairings, the group met to agree on a resolution, decide on the best rebuttals, attach rebuttal cards to the reason-counterargument card pairs, and to assume ownership of each of the card sets for the showdown.

Activity 9: Contemplating Mixed Evidence

The coach offered the team additional evidence material she had identified. This evidence included the full news articles from which the coach had taken only sections to show the team previously; at this point, the teams could see the full articles included paragraphs representing both sides, not just their own. Each of the articles thus included material that could be drawn on to support either side. The coach encouraged the team to consider how the opposing team would use the evidence, as well as how the evidence supported their position.

Activity 10: Conducting and Evaluating Two-Sided Arguments

As preparation for the showdown, the coach played the opposing side in reviewing argument-counterargument-rebuttal sequences. As final preparation, an opposing-team member joined the group for practice dialogs, which remaining team members critiqued.

The Showdown

The teams met with their coaches and an external judge (not from the school) who attended the session and reviewed the rules for the showdown. Each team chose who would speak for the team and when a new speaker would be substituted, with the proviso that no person would speak for more than three minutes and every person would speak at least once. At the request of any team member, the two teams could break into "huddles" to confer. The debate continued for twenty to thirty minutes, during which time everyone participated as a speaker and numerous huddles were called. At the conclusion, the judge announced that, before a team could be declared the winner, it would be necessary to conduct tie-breaking dialogs between pro-con pairs and these would be completed later that week.

Final Assessment

The dialogs between pairs and the individual arguments that had been conducted at the outset of the activity were repeated as a final assessment of skills. Insofar as possible, students engaged in dialogs with the same opposing partner they argued with as part of the initial assessment.

Beginning to Argue

There can be no doubt about one feature of our argument curriculum: It works. It gave students in disadvantaged schools who saw little purpose in school activities, including adolescents in juvenile detention, a reason to argue. The extrinsic rewards they were promised (a party or an outing) were minimal. Although those rewards gained the students' initial attention, students soon focused on winning the showdown, with little talk about why it was important to win.

Motivation increased, rather than flagged, as the program progressed. The activities succeeded in heightening interest in the opposing team's efforts, and the mystery around not having any contact with the opposing team led students to eagerly anticipate finally getting to talk to them. The possibility of eavesdropping on the other team (such as going into the room where they were meeting on some pretext) became a topic of conversation.

By the time the showdown took place, students were behaving as if something important was at stake. Intellectual energy was especially notable during the huddles. Stronger members of each team debated what would work best; and, if a weaker member was returning to the speaker's seat, he or she would be coached by stronger members regarding what to say.

Clearly, the program "works" as an exercise that holds students' interest.

But how does it fare with respect to engaging students in authentic argumentive discourse, the kind of discourse I have claimed is needed for students to discover the benefits of argument and to develop the skills it entails? Authentic discourse requires that participants talk to one another in meaningful ways, with each speaker's contribution shaped by what the preceding speaker has said. Skilled argumentive discourse, moreover, requires that the speaker address the claim that an opponent has made in a way that identifies its shortcomings and thereby reduces its force. This is the genuine counterargument that we noted increased in frequency when students engaged in authentic dialogic arguments with one another.

Dialogic Argument

We undertook similar analyses of the initial and final dialogs that students engaged in prior to and following the program described in this chapter. The trends we observed are in exactly the same directions that we observed in the studies described at the beginning of the chapter in which the intervention consisted only of a series of dyadic arguments with different peers. Overall, however, the effects are of greater magnitude.

Table 8.1 shows data for thirty-four eighth graders, from the struggling school and a neighboring school, reported on by Kuhn and Udell (2003). The comparison group noted in the table experienced only the first part of the curriculum (through developing reasons into an argument); they did not engage in discourse with peers holding opposing opinions. As a result, their progress was more limited, suggesting that argumentive discourse, and not simply participation in an activity involving the topic, is a critical aspect of the experience. Both groups progressed, however, and in the same directions as observed in the groups described earlier in this chapter. In two key categories—counterargument (against the other's claim) and clarification (of one's own position)—changes occurred in the anticipated directions. The percentage of talk devoted to argument against the other's position increased from the initial assessment prior to the activity to the final assessment that followed it. Conversely, percentage of talk devoted to exposition of arguers' own views decreased during this same period.

Boxes 8.1 and 8.2 offer a qualitative picture of these changes. Each box presents for comparison the initial dialog and then the final dialog, several months later, of one pair of students. Y and H's initial dialog was not really a dialog at all. They did no more than state their respective positions and leave them there, juxtaposed. S and G initially produced the kind of dialog in which the participants are satisfied to achieve a simple, practical resolution. The subsequent dialogs of each pair were significantly longer—both

Table 8.1. Initial and final average percentage use of two discourse types by adolescent participants in argument curriculum

Clarify

	Initial (%)	Final (%)
Main group	37.2	18.5
Comparison group	44.3	32.4

Counterargument

	Initial (%)	Final (%)
Main group	5.3	30.6
Comparison group	11.4	21.4

pairs had much more to say. But the dialogs also differed dramatically in quality from their earlier counterparts. The dialog itself took on a purpose, a direction, a life of its own. Although their arguments were largely situated in concrete, simplistic scenarios and were largely devoid of the sophisticated conceptual abstractions that are associated with skilled argument, their argumentive intent and strategy were clear.

H, for example, repeatedly made reference to the sense that his dialog with Y had a purpose; there was something to be achieved: "You're coming close to my point," he said, and later, "So that's good, but you still haven't caught up to my point." When H sought and was unable to obtain Y's agreement on a point, he resorted to a personal instance ("Let's say I killed your mother"). H had clear intention in introducing this instance; he was anticipating that Y would respond in a way that would give him argumentive advantage. (When Y did not, however, H was thrown off track and lost focus temporarily.) Similarly, Y, seeking to establish an inconsistency in H's position—a sophisticated argument strategy—said, "Remember that statement that you said." Despite momentary lapses in focus like H's, the dialog overall retained its integrity, and it is possible to follow the major thread of reasoning from beginning to end.

The dialog between Y and H is typical of what we observed in these middle-school students' final dialogs, rather than an exception. The features of the dialog between S and G (Box 8.2) are similar, although their dialog was even longer (it is not reproduced in its entirety here). At the outset, their intention was clear to establish points of agreement and disagreement. S said at one point, "That's true, but the point is . . ." Both S and G sought concessions on the part of the other, a key argument strategy. At one point G even

Box 8.1

INITIAL AND FINAL DIALOGS BETWEEN Y AND H

Initial Dialog

H: I am very much in favor of capital punishment. For one thing, like let's say like somebody murders somebody and that person gets a good lawyer and in like two or three months because he's on death row. And that lawyer could help him get off death row for like a good amount of money. And like another reason that like . . . well, I'm very much in favor, but sometimes I'm like, I'm not in favor because if my brother murdered somebody and I get put in jail for it, I don't want the highest capital punishment settlement because I didn't even do nothing. So I got two different feelings about it.

Y: Well, I'm against capital punishment because like one person could go on death row and they didn't really do it because it's another person and it says in the Bible thou shall not kill.

[dialog ends]

Final Dialog

Y: See, capital punishment is bad because everyone deserves a second chance. No one deserves to die like that.

H: But not in all cases you deserve a second chance because like, let's say you, like a person you don't know could come and they'll go and kill the president. You think they'll deserve a second chance? No. And then like let's say you do deserve a second chance after they done killed the president. They go out and kill the mayor, the governor, and everybody else, so.

Y: Yeah, but how they gonna go out and kill the mayor, the governor, when you got life imprisonment for that and solitary confinement.

H: Yeah. You're coming close to my point, because you're saying if you get life imprisonment you don't get a second chance when you get life imprisonment. Life imprisonment is like your third strike, so you're staying in there for good.

Y: Yeah, but that having the killer, like instead of just dying for it just like that, you, they have a chance to think about what they done and they want to be forgiven for that.

H: Not all the time, cause let's say if I was to go over to your house and kill your mother. You think you would forgive me for that? No. So let's say I killed your mother and everybody else in your family and you was the only one left and you would have to go to a foster home. You would want me to get capital punishment, right?

Y: No, because I would forgive you because . . . it's like this. [pause] Darn, I forgot what I was about to say. Go ahead until I remember what I was about to say.

H: Well, I would . . . if I was in your shoes right now. I wouldn't forgive you because you killing blood right there. So I would try and come out and kill you myself and give you capital punishment my way.

Y: Two wrongs don't make a right. And besides it doesn't bring the victim back. You just have to forgive and forget.

H: But not all the time because let's say you was younger and you was like four years old. And I killed everybody in your family. Let's say I was a grown up. I killed everybody and you four years old. Wouldn't you want your mother to teach you all of the girl things there is to know? You want nobody else to teach you but your mother because you would feel more safe talking to your mother than pure strangers, right?

Y: Yeah, but . . .

H: Okay. So you would want me to get capital punishment so you don't gotta see my dirty face again. Cause I killed your whole family. Am I right or wrong?

Y: Well, it all depends. Like I still got my aunt. I still got my grandmother, alright.

H: I killed everyone in your family. You the only one left. You gotta go to a foster home.

Y: Well, not exactly. I mean there's a way that if your mother had a will, right. And she wrote something down that said that you were her clos-est friend. You didn't say about killing any closest friend. And capital punishment, you need note that even though the killer, I mean the victim, is six feet under the ground, right. I mean the victim is never coming back, okay. And what about the family of the killer? I mean they are gonna be sad too, okay.

H: So you would want me to have, you would rather me have life in prison than capital punishment? Or capital punishment over life in prison?

Y: Life imprisonment. I mean you have to like think about the other fam-ily. I'm not gonna like go out and then just say, oh kill the killer, kill him. Alright, I have to think about it first. I have to put myself in the killer's family's shoes, see how they're suffering.

H: But that's true. But you can't also depend on that because I can have life in prison and I could only be twenty two years old and let's say I live till eighty. By the time I get to like thirty or thirty five, they'll bring my case back up into the court and if I get a fair trial and I got a good lawyer like Johnny Cochran or somebody, I can get off life im-prisonment and go on parole. Or I could be under house arrest until they find out that. I could be living on the street. Like let's say I say that I didn't mean to kill your family. I thought somebody gave me the wrong address and I just came in there and I started blazing. You wouldn't be able to say that, right?

Y: Right.

H: So you wouldn't want me to die because you don't want no second chances coming. You be like, oh since you gave me life imprisonment, since I'm out of jail I'm gonna try to kill you. That's what you're giving that person a chance to do. Trying to get revenge on what the person did to them.

Y: Some capital punishment is also wrong because they could pick an innocent person for the killer. I mean we read that it took 16 years to find out this man was innocent and it was the day before the man was going to death row.

H: So let's say the same thing happens to me. That man was still in life imprisonment until like somebody brought the case back into court and they find out, oh I'm gonna give you capital punishment if I find out you ain't innocent.

Y: Now the article said that he was going to capital punishment until these students from college like found some research stating that the man was innocent. The man doesn't have that much mentality to find out that he couldn't even kill because his IQ was 50. And the gunman used his left hand and he writes with his right.

H: So that's good, but you still haven't caught up to my point yet. Would you rather have that person get another chance to kill you or would you rather that person just die right there?

Y: That all depends. I mean what about if you felt sorry for him?

H: But you can't feel sorry for that person because you killed . . . I killed your whole family. So what would you rather do? Would you rather me have capital punishment or life imprisonment? So if I get life imprisonment, I still get to see my family . . . I get to do whatever I want in jail. I get to play basketball, go outside, see the ground. I get to sleep on a comfy bed. Where's everybody else that you love? Six feet underground.

Y: But not exactly. Remember that statement that you said. You get to see your family. I mean they have solitary confinement, so. You don't get to see your family. You don't eat with anybody, you eat by yourself. You're in this dark room for life, so.

H: But I'm still alive. So I get to speak to myself. I'm still alive because you make a stupid move by not putting me on capital punishment.

Y: Two wrongs don't make a right, though.

H: Sometimes they do. Let's say me and you are brother and sister and we got a littler brother. If I kill somebody and you kill somebody and the little brother sees us getting in trouble, don't you think he will learn

from our mistakes, not to do that? So two wrongs make a right sometimes. And that's not always true.

Y: But most of the time it doesn't.

H: I know that's true, too.

Box 8.2

INITIAL AND FINAL DIALOGS BETWEEN S AND G

Initial Dialog

G: What do you think about capital punishment?

S: I would go with it because if you do a crime, you should pay for it.

G: But I think that nobody's life should be taken away, and if they do
something bad they should stay in jail for the rest of their life and suffer.

S: Not even if it's a major, major crime, you don't feel that they should?

G: No they should stay in jail and suffer, like life.

S: For life? I can go with that.

G: See, if you had killed somebody, would you want to die by capital punishment?

S: No, I'd rather stay in jail for life.

G: Thank you. See, that's my answer.

S: Me too.

Final Dialog Excerpt

G: Capital punishment is bad because it does not bring the victim back
and it does not make the family feel better.

S: Well, I agree with you with the fact that . . .

G: Then you just said you agree with me.

S: No. No, not completely. I agree with you in the way that it doesn't
bring the victim back. But I disagree with you that it won't make the
family feel better. Cause I feel yes it will, because this family will feel
that justice has been served. And basically we aren't giving capital punishment or trying to enforce capital punishment to bring the victim
back. But we are enforcing it so that the person will receive their
justified punishment for taking another innocent human.

G: I disagree with you about that the family will feel better. The family
won't feel better. The family regret about that victim, not the person
that killed him. The family could care less about that person dying or
not. The family just wants the victim back.

S: Yes, of course. That's a natural feeling. If some one of your relatives dies, of course you will want the victim back. But you will also be angry at the fact that your innocent family member was killed for no apparent reason from the psychopath on the street. And then you would want justice.

G: Let's say if you kill some boy named Kareem, right? And his family was so mad. Would you want to get capital punishment? Or would you want to stay in jail for the rest of your life and suffer?

S: Well, a normal . . . well, basically . . .

G: No, you wouldn't.

S: No, I didn't answer that. Um, let's see. How would I feel?

G: You'll feel that you should stay in jail for the rest of your life and suffer.

S: Well, me being the person . . .

G: Cause for you being killed right there and now, that's not suffering. But you can suffer for a life sentence in jail and be in solitary confinement and don't see your family for the rest of your life. You just be in a big hole.

S: Well, I feel that of course I would want jail time because I killed the person. That's just a normal instinct. If you kill somebody, you don't want to be killed, because you're still a human. Every human wants to live. So.

G: Yeah, but they're like . . .

S: Of course it would be me to want to live and stay in jail, rather than being killed, but that . . .

G: Thank you!

S: That doesn't make it right.

G: I'm saying but it doesn't make it right to kill somebody else and keep on making a cycle. That is like committing a crime yourself. And you're taking a life and God doesn't like that. And the Bible says thou shall not kill anyone.

S: That's true, but the point is . . .

G: Intentionally.

S: The point is that the criminal killed somebody.

G: I'm saying but . . .

S: And I understand what you're saying. It's killing another life. But what about that person who killed that person who's now dead? And since they're a killer mentally and can do so physically, they can go out and kill another person.

G: I'm saying . . .

S: So that would be two people killed.

G: I'm saying but the criminal could've made a mistake. People need a second chance. A second chance.

S: But, see, you need to define what your second chance means. Is your second chance meaning to go out . . .

G: A second chance means . . .

S: And change your way of life and do what's right?

G: No, a second . . .

S: Or is it a second chance to go out and kill a second person?

G: A second chance is a life sentence. He's not going back outside. It's a life sentence. Nowhere, you know.

S: But in these facilities where they stay . . . Because in jail are there not other people in there, other criminals?

G: But I'm saying they be in the hole where people is not around them. They eat in that hole, they is always in that hole.

S: But who brings them the food? People. There's always someone.

G: No, people don't bring them in the hole. It's a little like belt-thing and you just slide the thing right through.

S: It's not possible for one human being to live in a hole without having some human or person go there and communicate.

G: No people, no.

S: Well, first of all, capital punishment is good anyway because it reduces crime.

G: No, it don't reduce crime. No it don't. We got the facts, but I don't have it with me right now.

S: I know where, in a place called Philips, eleven . . .

G: That's only one state.

S: That's one state and I have a list of other ones. But just to use this one as an example . . .

G: It's not a good example.

S: Um, before capital punishment was enforced in that state, the crimes are high. But they say that after they enforced capital punishment the crimes reduced.

G: It was . . .

S: Therefore so the same way it can do it in a lot of other states as well and save a lot of other people in other states.

G: Probably was a coincidence.

S: Oh boy. So you're telling me that capital punishment will not reduce crime in any way?

G: It will not. It's going to stay the same.

S: But it's been shown that it didn't stay the same.

G: I'm saying like people don't think before they kill. We all know that. They don't plan like that.

[A lengthy discussion ensues on whether criminals think before they act, with S and G each offering contrasting instances to support their view. They return briefly to the question of the degree of suffering prisoners experience in jail, and then go on to consider the role of capital punishment as a deterrent.]

G: How do they know they're going to get caught or not? A lot of criminals say, "I'm not getting caught if I kill this person."

S: Yeah, but if they see that somebody else who almost . . . if they commit a crime and somebody else who killed somebody else. If they see somebody receiving capital punishment, I think that would make you think twice of if I should kill this person.

G: I don't think. Those people are crazy. They probably don't think about that stuff.

S: Excuse me. Everybody thinks, crazy or not. Insane or sane, you have to think. And of course if you see some . . . When you were little and your parents told you not to do something and you did it anyway and you got a punishment, you remembered not to do it again. Why? Because you had already received the punishment. Now these people are looking on TV and seeing these people getting killed and punished for what they did. You think, "Wow, I don't want to die, so let me straighten out."

G: They don't think like that.

S: How do you know if they think like that or not?

G: I know. Cause we have facts about that.

S: Excuse me. We're humans okay and . . .

G: Humans make mistakes too.

S: Humans have this tendency. If you see somebody receive a punishment for something they did. Tell me there's not a little hesitation In your mind. "Well, let's weigh this out. Should I do it and receive that? Or should I not do it and go on a clean slate?" Most of the time they'll think about it and say, "No, I don't want to do that because I don't want to end up where that person is."

G: I don't think so, because how do they know if they're gonna get caught or not?

S: Okay. (Sighs, in resignation).

said, "Thank you!" after he had won a concession from S. Later S asserted, "You need to define what your second chance means," and it is clear that she had a purpose in making this demand for definition so common among skilled arguers. Questions of fact are relevant to the argument. G at one point rejected S's previous statement—"It's not a good example"—and later S challenged, "How do you know if they think like that or not?" We also saw S employ an analogy (of parent and child), a sophisticated strategy intended to persuade G of her point.

Felton and Kuhn (2001) identify specific argument strategies that are seen in skilled argumentive discourse and the frequency with which they appear in the dialogs of young adolescents and young adults. The discourse skills displayed in the dialogs of Y and H and S and G are clearly far from perfected. In both dialogs, the discussion frequently meandered. And even when directly addressing the opponent's preceding statement, the speaker was likely to offer an alternative argument that did not directly criticize the opponent's argument rather than a genuine counterargument. The participants' ideas about the topic remained unsophisticated, and the manner in which they expressed them was certainly concrete and unsophisticated. Still, the level of discourse skill we observed was impressive. If the objective is to build argument skills, their performance is truly something to build on.

As important as the argument strategies themselves is the fact that each of the student's contributions to the dialog tells us that the participants had a sense that they were engaged in a joint, purposeful undertaking, coproducing an intellectual product that consisted of far more than the juxtaposition of their respective positions. They would not have gone to the effort to employ the various discourse strategies we saw unless they had a concept of argument as requiring more than having an opinion superior to that of one's opponent. Instead, they had begun to see the point of arguing.

Individual Argument

Is the same growth evident in students' individual arguments? These are of course important to look at in light of our claim that dialogic argument is the most fruitful context in which to develop individual argument skills. Does the social context in which students are able to engage and practice their argument skills externalize individual thinking in a way that strengthens it and, if so, does this enhanced strength remain apparent when thinking once again becomes covert?

The answer is largely yes. Students' individual arguments for or against capital punishment also improved in quality, based on the system of analysis presented in Box 8.3. Overall, participants offered new reasons at the final assessment and excluded some of the reasons they gave at the initial assessment. The reasons that were dropped from initial to final assessment were typically lower-level reasons (levels II and III in Box 8.3), whereas new reasons added at the later assessment were typically higher-level reasons (level I).

Box 8.3

LEVELS OF INDIVIDUAL ARGUMENTS FOR AND AGAINST CAPITAL PUNISHMENT

Pro Arguments

I. Functional arguments
  A. Alternatives to capital punishment are ineffective or less effective than capital punishment
  A1. Alternatives to capital punishment are not effective as deterrents
  A2. Alternatives to capital punishment are not effective in protecting society from criminals
  A3. Alternatives to capital punishment are not sufficient punishment
  A4. Alternatives to capital punishment fail to rehabilitate criminals
  A5. Alternatives to capital punishment are too burdensome or costly a way to serve their purpose
  B. Capital punishment reduces crime
  B1. Capital punishment deters people from crime
  B2. Capital punishment protects society from the acts of criminals
  C. Capital punishment is an appropriate punishment
  C1. Eye-for-eye
  C2. Criminals have forfeited the right to life and privileges associated with it
  C3. Compensates victim or victim's family

II. Nonfunctional arguments (focused on conditions that make capital punishment justified, without consideration of its functions)
  A. Capital punishment is justified only if guilt is established beyond reasonable doubt
  B. Capital punishment is justified only if criminal judged competent to be responsible for own actions
  C. Capital punishment is justified only if it is applied consistently
  D. Capital punishment is justified only if the crime is sufficiently grave
  E. Capital punishment is justified only in the case of repeated crime

III. Nonjustificatory arguments
  A. Justification based on sentiment
  B. Appeal to precedent (capital punishment has been in use for a long time)
  C. Appeal to majority (many or most think it's a good idea)
  D. Appeal to authority (without intervening argument)
  E. Crime exists and needs a remedy

Con Arguments

I. Functional arguments
   A. Alternatives exist that are preferable to capital punishment
   A1. Alternatives to capital punishment are better as deterrents
   A2. Alternatives to capital punishment are better in protecting society from criminals
   A3. Alternatives to capital punishment are better punishment
   A4. Alternatives to capital punishment allow rehabilitation of criminals
   B. Capital punishment does not reduce crime or reduce it sufficiently
   B1. Capital punishment is not effective in deterring people from crime
   B2. Capital punishment is not effective in protecting society from the acts of criminals
   C. Capital punishment is not an appropriate punishment
   C1. Capital punishment commits the same crime it is meant to punish
   C2. Capital punishment does not right the wrong (doesn't restore loss to victim of crime)
   C3. We lack the right to take life
   C4. We lack the right to make judgments of who should live or die
   C5. We lack the right to make judgments of other people's actions
   C6. Capital punishment violates the principle of forgiveness
   C7. Any killing is wrong
   C8. Capital punishment is violent, barbaric
   C9. Capital punishment wastes lives
   C10. Capital punishment serves no purpose
   C11. Enforcers of capital punishment themselves commit crime

II. Nonfunctional arguments (focused on possibly remediable defects in administration of capital punishment, without consideration of its functions)
   A. Capital punishment may punish innocent people
   B. Capital punishment may punish people who are not responsible for their actions
   C. Capital punishment is not administered uniformly (may be discriminatory against certain groups)
   D. Capital punishment may punish people who committed crime accidentally or as victim of circumstances
   E. Capital punishment is not administered efficiently (e.g., may be drawn out and costly)

III. Nonjustificatory arguments
   A. Justification based on sentiment
   B. Appeal to precedent (capital punishment has not been widely used or as widely used as it once was)
   C. Appeal to majority (many or most are against capital punishment)
   D. Appeal to authority (without intervening argument)

From Kuhn, Shaw, and Felton, Effects of dyadic interaction on argumentive reasoning. *Cognition and Instruction, 1997, 15(3)*, 287–315.

The following example portrays one student's progress:

Initial assessment: If someone did something wrong, they should be subject to capital punishment. (Why is that?) Because for instance if they kill someone, maybe the same thing is due to them. (Any other reason?) Well, I feel that people should pay if they did something wrong.

Final assessment: If someone goes out and kills another person they should receive a justified punishment, an equal punishment. So that if they killed someone then they should receive the same thing. But I can also see how other people can have a different opinion because not everyone thinks the same and they may feel that it's wrong to kill another person, that people deserve a second chance. But personally I feel that if you have enough nerve to go out and kill somebody else, well then you just deserve to be killed as well. (Okay, anything else?) Well, one of the reasons why I have this opinion is that I've seen where facts have shown that capital punishment has reduced crime. And I always think that less crime will make a better life for everyone.

This initial individual argument in favor of capital punishment appeared in Chapter 7. It appears here together with the subsequent individual argument. Over time, we see, the argument became two-sided, richer, and more qualified.

From Winning to Knowing

The emergence of a dialogic dimension in individual arguments supports the claim that the two kinds of argument are closely related. The point is an important one, for the claim that a dynamic, dialogic approach is the best way to support the development of skilled argument rests on this relationship. The externalization that discourse offers allows the structure of argument to become visible—and with the scaffold that our index cards provided, even tangible. If students learn to engage in this discourse covertly—to conduct both sides of a conversation inside their heads—their thinking is more likely to take on the disciplined, directed character of what is so widely referred to, but vaguely defined, as critical thinking. Thinking as argument (Kuhn, 1991, 1992; Yeh, 2002) offers a way to define what we mean by critical thinking. Dialogic argument, we have suggested, offers the most effective support for its development.

Situating this activity in a goal-based, or project-based, context draws on ideas that go back at least as far as John Dewey. Dewey (1916) described five conditions for effective educational experience that have remarkable applicability in the early years of the next century:

> [*first*, that] there be a continuous activity in which [the student] is interested for its own sake; *secondly*, that a genuine problem develop within this situation as a stimulus to thought; *third*, that he possess the information and make the observations needed to deal with it; *fourth*, that suggested solutions occur to him which he shall be responsible for developing in an orderly way; *fifth*, that he have the opportunity and occasion to test his ideas by application, to make their meaning clear and to discover for himself their validity (p. 170).

It makes a good deal of sense that these are conditions that support productive educational activity, for they are also conditions likely to prevail when individuals choose undertakings they will devote themselves to in their lives beyond school. People most often have a purpose when they invest themselves in a demanding activity. They typically do not work hard without knowing why they are doing so.

Arguing about a complex social issue like capital punishment involves negotiating opposing claims whose comparative merit can be evaluated only in a framework of alternatives and evidence. A framework of this sort requires sustained cognitive effort to construct, refine, and negotiate. The relatively late developing evaluativist epistemology outlined in Chapter 2 is needed to fully support this effort. Neither the absolutist nor the multiplist epistemology that precedes it offers any reason to argue.

Evidence described in this chapter indicates that middle-school students who display little academic motivation or accomplishment can develop argumentive discourse skills as a result of participation in a goal-based activity. But do they gain a more mature understanding of the epistemological foundations of argument? Do they come to recognize a point to arguing beyond being the winner of the argument?

The only possible answer is incompletely, at best. All of the students in our research were able, by the end of their participation, to generate counterarguments to their classmates' claims. But they did not do so consistently. They had trouble sustaining this high level of argument strategy and often lost focus and drifted off course. Counterarguments to counterarguments—rebuttals—occurred at a much lower level of frequency than they do in expert discourse (Felton and Kuhn, 2001). To further develop these skills, these students, like most of their peers, need opportunities to practice dialogic argument over a wide range of issues and content and occasions.

Yet as a result of their involvement in this dialogic exercise, students clearly developed a richer understanding surrounding the topic of capital punishment, despite the fact that none of them began with much knowledge about the topic. By engaging one another's ideas in a genuine, deep way, these students co-constructed knowledge that none of them had previously. As a result, their involvement served to illustrate to them the fruits of authentic argument. These fruits can be appreciated only through personal experience; telling students has little value. If students go on to engage in similar experiences with other topics, they stand to acquire a deeper sense of why they are doing so and what they can gain. They may still want to win, but that will no longer be their only purpose. They will be on their way to understanding reasoned discourse as the most powerful means of evaluating competing ideas and constructing shared understanding. They will have constructed an understanding of argument itself.

Wherever students are on this path toward mastery, the skills and understanding associated with argument are truly ones that will equip them for life, not just for more school. In this sense, our own better understanding of this path and the milestones along it can contribute to the construction of a more satisfactory definition of what it means to become educated. I turn to this question in the next chapter.

CONCLUSIONS | IV

BECOMING EDUCATED | 9

What does it mean to be an educated person? The question is central to what goes on in the educational world. It defines the goals of the educational process and the criteria for judging how well they've been met. If an accepted test or credential can identify those we wish to call educated, otherwise very difficult questions are avoided. An educated person is one who has passed a certain exam or obtained a certain degree. The degree or credential becomes the objective of education. Achieving it means that the goal of becoming educated has been met. If, on the other hand, we maintain that being educated encompasses something more, or more subtle, than what available credentials can document, clear-cut answers to questions of educational mission disappear, replaced by uncertainty and, very often, heated debate.

A goal of this book has been to address the need for better answers to the question of what it means to be educated. Seeking answers to this question brings us back to the question, What should education achieve? Consistent with the proposed objective of developing the mind's capabilities as the best preparation for life, I propose two broad components as central to the definition of an educated person. One has to do with intellectual skills and the other with intellectual values. An educated person is one who is capable of certain kinds of activities of an intellectual nature. At least as important, an educated person is one who values these things as worth doing. In this chapter, I consider each component in turn.

Intellectual Skills

The preceding chapters feature two broad categories of intellectual skills—skills of inquiry and skills of argument. I propose these skills as a foundation on which becoming educated rests. The first question to be asked is why inquiry and argument deserve this exalted place in a hierarchy of intellectual skills, above other potential candidates.

Why Inquiry and Argument?

Two major justifications can be offered for according inquiry and argument this status. First, the value and utility of these skills are found in life, not just in school. Education must prepare students for life beyond school, and inquiry and argument are broad and powerful skills that students take with them outside the classroom and well beyond their school years. Their exercise leaves people enriched, individually and collectively. They are social skills, employed collaboratively in pursuit of shared goals at least as often as solitary ones.

Second, the value of inquiry and argument is intrinsic and revealed as the skills are engaged, practiced, and perfected. These are not skills someone acquires on faith because an external authority has deemed them a means to some unrelated end. Inquiry and argument yield their own rewards. They are means to the end of knowing, and the educated person has come to value knowing as preferable to ignorance, and hence as capable of serving as its own reward.

Even if we grant inquiry and argument these characteristics, do they really trump all of the many other kinds of intellectual skills that can be identified? Are there not other intellectual skills at least as important in their contribution to productive adult life? Literacy skills, for example, come to mind as a prime candidate. At least the first four or five years of universal schooling are given over largely to literacy objectives, and the education of those who fail to achieve these literacy goals largely comes to a standstill.

But literacy for what? Every child must make the critical transition from learning to read to reading to learn. To truly make this transition and become a lifelong reader, the developing reader must come to appreciate the purpose of reading as one of finding out. Once they leave school and the reading demands it imposes, adults continue to read only if they have come to believe that there are worthwhile things to find out and that the printed word is an effective medium for finding them out. And this, of course, brings us squarely back to inquiry. Neither reading nor writing is an end in itself. Both are effortful, energy-consuming endeavors that are undertaken in the service of a further goal, the goal of finding out and knowing. A similar argument can be made that any number of other, more specific kinds of intellectual skills are ones that serve these same ends of learning and knowing.

What About Knowledge?

Chapter 1 examines other goals of education, ones that might serve to define the educated person. Arguably mastery of a particular body of knowledge should be the goal, for example, whether acquired through a teacher's instruction or one's own inquiry. Is it not the product, rather than the process, that matters in the end and identifies people as educated?

But the question immediately arises, which knowledge? Certainly an educated person will have acquired considerable knowledge. Should we try to specify which or how much knowledge qualifies one to be considered educated? The "culture wars" (Graff, 1992) have made clear the difficulty of fulfilling this task to everyone's satisfaction. Is there a better alternative?

If students have developed the skills enabling them to acquire knowledge effectively, as well as the values that accompany these skills, it is unlikely they will fail to use them. Why, then, not regard students as competent to choose the questions they wish to ask and the kinds of knowledge they wish to obtain? Beyond potential benefits to the student, this solution has one decided advantage: It avoids the troublesome question of who is to decree what knowledge others ought to acquire.

What are the implications of this solution for defining what it means to be educated? They are profound: The definition is cast not in terms of achievement but in terms of potential. People are not regarded as educated based on whether they have knowledge of topic X—Greek civilization, say. Rather, a mark of the educated person is the recognition that there are others who have found it worthwhile knowing about such topics, together with the skills and confidence to seek and secure such knowledge themselves should they wish to do so. Becoming educated, then, means achieving the skills and values that confer an unlimited capacity and inclination to learn and to know.

And what about the hypothetical student who fulfills only part of this definition, by developing knowledge-acquisition skills but showing no inclination to use them? Educators continue to debate the most effective strategies for inspiring such students. But stipulating exactly what the student must learn would probably not be one of these strategies, even if we were able to reach agreement on the subject matter to be mastered.

Should we have no concern at all, then, about what particular knowledge students acquire? Another way to frame this question is to ask where inquiry and argument skills fit in the larger school curriculum, a question we turn to shortly. A preliminary answer is that we should seek to develop the intellectual skills of inquiry and argument in such a way that they will become a framework that is brought to any learning. When students approach a new area of inquiry, we would like them to seek answers to several questions as a matter of course: *What can I claim and how do I know? What do I not know and need to find out? What are the claims and counterclaims at stake here, and what are the arguments for and against each?*

The orientation we would like to see develop is well decribed by Deborah Meier (1995), who claims that being well educated means "getting in the habit of developing theories that can be articulated clearly and then checked out in a thoughtful way" (p. 155). Meier's prescription certainly invokes the skills of inquiry and argument; but in also invoking what she calls "habits of mind," she recognizes that skills are only part of the story. Students must be disposed to use these skills. The term *habit*, however, has the unfortunate connotation that a person can get used to engaging in the activity in a mechanical, effortless way. Rigorous thinking is never effortless. Learning, properly understood as change in understanding, entails purposeful investment of time and energy. Students will be disposed to use the intellectual skills they have developed only if they believe doing so will produce knowledge they deem worth having. I turn shortly to the values that support such a disposition. The implication for now is that we cannot tell students exactly what to learn because we cannot take over for them the process of deciding what is worth knowing.

Is Skill Development General or Context-Specific?

The educational goals proposed here are useful only to the extent we can answer the practical question that any educator is right to ask: How do we do it? Here, the position I take is controversial. Intellectual-skill objectives, educators are likely to recommend, should always be situated in a specific context of rich knowledge goals. Skills develop most effectively, many claim, when exercised in the pursuit of meaningful knowledge; to pursue skill development apart from such specific knowledge-acquisition contexts is at best difficult and probably doomed to failure.

I find this position unduly strong and lacking in empirical substantiation. Certainly, knowledge acquisition must be "situated"—any student learns about something specific in a certain context and for his or her particular purposes. Students do not acquire intellectual skills as abstract competencies. Young children, for example, only acquire categorization or measurement skills to the extent that they have things to categorize or measure. It does not follow, however, that intellectual skills cannot be *identified* outside of specific contexts, in their more general, content-independent form. Indeed, the previous chapters demonstrate that they can and, moreover, that doing so is central to understanding their nature and development. Doing so is also central to educational practice. To have much hope of success as educators, we need to understand, in the most general form possible, exactly what the competencies are that we wish to see develop.

Does it follow that students who acquire these skills can immediately apply them to any suitable content? This is a question to be answered by empirical research, and the answer has come back a definitive no. Skills emerge first only under limited conditions of high external support and are only gradually extended to a wider range of contexts and more flexible, unsupported use (Fischer and Bidell, 1991). Demonstrations of context-specificity in the appearance of cognitive skills have led some to the extreme view that skills are entirely context-specific. A skill, in other words, resides one hundred percent in the specific social context in which it is practiced—a view associated with the sociocultural school of thought (Rogoff, 1998)—and not at all as a more general entity in the repertory of the person who uses it. Such a view, in its extreme form, largely obliterates the concept of skill itself, defined as potential behavior characteristic of an individual, because it attributes behavior to the situation, not to the individual. The more moderate position, and the one best supported by current research, lies in the middle ground between generality and specificity. Intellectual skills do exist as identifiable competencies in the repertory of an individual, although their emergence and use are shaped by specific experience.

The still different and critical questions we can now turn to are the pedagogical ones: How should the skills in question be developed? Should learning contexts be "knowledge rich" or "knowledge lean"? Here we might be asking either of two questions. One is whether contexts for learning skills ought to be knowledge rich. The other is whether knowledge goals should be incorporated in efforts to foster skill development.

The answer to the first question is an unqualified yes. No learning context should ever be stripped of meaningful content. The historical example of psychologists' asking people to learn associations between nonsense syllables (pef/lar), a popular research paradigm in the 1950s, makes this clear. Researchers of this era thought that stripping the material to be learned of any prior meaning would enable them to study the learning process in a pure, uncontaminated form. The outcome, in a word, was that researchers found out a great deal about how people learn associations between nonsense syllables, but the relevance of these observations to how people learn meaningful material in real-life contexts has remained dubious.

To the second question—whether knowledge goals should be incorporated in efforts to promote skill development—I propose the more controversial answer of no. Teachers typically have many and varied knowledge goals for their students, ones that at best only partially overlap with students' own goals. Teachers' knowledge goals are most often worthy and deserving of attention (although they are the topic of a different book from this one). How can these knowledge goals be respected while fostering skill development?

My position is that both sets of goals—knowledge goals and skill goals—

are complex, and educators therefore generally should not attempt to situate skill development in the context of ambitious knowledge goals. It is not necessary, and unduly challenging, to adopt the dual purpose of achieving both within a single learning context. Ample opportunities exist to pursue both. Skill development, especially in its early phases, requires focused attention, as an objective in its own right. Once skill development has progressed sufficiently, we hope that students will be able to bring the skills they have developed to any new learning situation. The objective is thus to acquire the skills in a robust, generalized form but also to develop a framework—a way of thinking—that learners will be disposed to bring to any new learning they undertake.

Intellectual Values

The question of learners' dispositions brings us to the topic of intellectual values. Students decide what is worth their while to invest effort in. Educators ignore students' intellectual values at their own risk.

Making Sense

Students develop their own ideas of what education and learning are about, even if the adults around them appear to ignore the question. And students act on these ideas. Or they fail to act. If they are not convinced of the value of intellectual skills that have been promoted in school, they will apply them in school only when required to do so and not anywhere else. And knowledge they acquire in school that remains unconnected to any reasons for knowing it will surely be quickly forgotten.

And so, in this respect, students hold all the cards. They, not those who teach them, determine what they will learn and know. We must, as a result, pay close attention to their sense-making, to what they think they are doing. For this will turn out to be of much greater importance than what we think we want to teach them.

Learning in Partnership

Attuned to students' sense-making efforts, educators should seek to enlist students as partners in their own education. Students need to become sold on the idea of school and its purposes. They need to become convinced that we are not wasting their time. They must see how and why what they are engaging in makes sense and understand where it leads. Only then will they regard the adults in their school lives as partners in an enterprise they have bought into.

If the partnership ideal is achieved, the adult's role becomes critical in multiple ways. By serving as guide, or coach, as students engage in shared activities, the adults who introduce and facilitate the activity demonstrate their own belief in its value. The student trusts the adult not to waste the time of either of them. This display of adult commitment is as important to students as the experience gained from the activity itself. What we ask students to do tells them what we as adults believe is worth doing. What we ask students to learn tells them what we believe is worth knowing.

It follows that we need to be very careful about what we ask students to do or learn. More is being learned than meets the eye. We can refer to this hidden curriculum as the metacurriculum.

The Metacurriculum

Consider the excerpt of text in Box 9.1, taken from the seventh-grade American history text used in Mrs. O's class at the best-practice school. Implicit in this text is a powerful subtext about what kinds of questions are important and what other kinds are not. Included in the subtext are numerous messages that certain things are not worth wondering about. By contrast, the questions that appear at the bottom of the page convey an explicit message that these are the points worth noting and remembering. And the final question, the question for "thinking about"—why do you think women found more opportunities to work outside the home during the war?—conveys that this is the most (possibly even the only) thought-worthy issue that the events described pose. Why, we might ask, this and not any of the alternatives posed in Box 9.2? The message that none of the kinds of questions posed in Box 9.2 is worth worrying about is far-reaching and no less powerful because it is conveyed in implicit rather than explicit form.

If the questions asked or not asked can have such a powerful effect, of potentially even greater impact are the kinds of activities that teachers communicate are worth, or not worth, doing. If teachers are accepted as partners in a shared enterprise, all those involved understand that teachers will ask the students to engage only in those activities that further their mutual goals. But this powerful adult role must be handled with extreme care. Students must be able to quickly discover the value of such activities for themselves, or any trust that has developed between teacher and student will very quickly dissipate. In this case, discovery is the only viable learning method. It is thus crucial that the activities that students engage in have the critical characteristics emphasized earlier. They must be activities of clearly evident intrinsic value, and this value must reveal itself as the requisite skills are engaged, practiced, and perfected.

Box 9.1
_____

EXCERPT FROM A SEVENTH-GRADE AMERICAN HISTORY TEXTBOOK

From Chapter 4, "Life in Wartime," A History of the Republic, vol. 1: U.S. to 1877 (Prentice-Hall). Excerpts from pages 403–408.

Troops on both sides were very young men. Most were under 21 years old. But war quickly changed raw recruits into tough veterans . . . They slept on the ground in rain and snow. They scavenged for food, water, and firewood . . . Boys of 18 learned to stand firm while cannon blasts shook the earth and bullets whizzed past their ears.

At times, Rebs and Yanks could be friendly enemies. Before one battle, a Confederate hailed a Union soldier with "Say Yank, got something to trade?" After swapping Union coffee for southern tobacco, the soldiers shook hands. "Good luck, Yank," said the Southerner. "I hope you won't get hurt in any of our fights."

Soldiers returned to the horrors of combat quickly. New technology made Civil War battles deadly . . . New cannons could hurl exploding shells several miles. In any battle, one quarter or more of the soldiers were casualties . . .

In one battle, Union troops knew that they were facing almost certain death. Each soldier wrote his name on a slip of paper and pinned it to his uniform. The soldiers wanted their bodies to be identified when the battle was over.

Soldiers who were sick, wounded, or captured faced different horrors. Medical care in the field was crude. Surgeons cut off the arms and legs of wounded men . . . over half the wounded died. And disease killed more men than bullets did. Prisoners of war on both sides suffered from disease and starvation.

. . .the Union was so desperate for soldiers that Congress passed a draft law in 1863 . . . the draft law allowed a man to avoid going into the army by paying $300 or by hiring someone to serve in his place. This angered many common people . . . Many draftees deserted . . .

some Northerners felt that they were being forced to fight to end slavery. Riots broke out in several cities. The worst riot, in New York City, lasted for four days in July 1863. White workers turned their anger against free blacks. They brutally murdered almost 100 blacks.

President Lincoln tried to stop anti-draft riots and other "disloyal practices." Several times, he denied the right to have a trial before being jailed. To those who protested his action, Lincoln quoted the Constitution. It gave him the right, he said, to deny people their rights "when in the cases of rebellion or invasion, the public safety may require it.". . .

In some ways, the Civil War helped the northern economy . . . Wartime demand for clothing, shoes, guns, ammunition, and other supplies brought a boom to these industries. Some people made fortunes by profiteering. Profiteers overcharged the government for supplies desperately needed for the war . . .

Women played vital roles on both sides during the war. As men left for the battlefields, women took over jobs in industry, in teachiing, and on farms. They help bake sales, donated jewelry, and organized fairs to raise money for medical supplies. Some women disguised themselves as soldiers and fought in battle. Others served as spies.

Section Review

1. Define: bounty, draft, habeas corpus, inflation, profiteer, tax-in-kind, civilian.
2. Why did support for the war decrease in the North? What did each side do to get more soldiers?
3. Why did the Confederate constitution create problems for Jefferson Davis?
4. How did each side raise money for the war?
5. What do you think? Why do you think women found more opportunities to work outside the home during the war?

Box 9.2

EDUCATION AS A PROCESS OF LEARNING THAT LIFE INVOLVES STRANGE THINGS THAT ARE NOT TO BE QUESTIONED

Questions the Text Does Not Ask

Why do we have wars? Can they be avoided?
Why are young males, rather than young females or older people, most often the participants in wars?
Can a superior justify sending his men to certain death?
Why wasn't medical care better?
How should prisoners of war be treated?
Should citizens be required to serve in the army?
    Should there be exceptions?
    Should wealthier citizens be able to pay substitutes to serve?
    Why did disagreement about Army service turn whites against blacks?
What moral issues does profiteering raise?
    Is it surprising that profiteers behave as they do?
Were most people in favor of the war?
    Did women have different feelings about the war than men did?

Inquiry and argument have just these characteristics. Students can find immediate meaning in them and can continue to make sense of them as they are engaged. But students must do the meaning-making work. Only through their own experience will students come to believe in inquiry and reasoned argument as offering the best means of evaluating competing claims, resolving conflicts, solving problems, and achieving goals. These are the intellectual values they need to develop. Developing these values is every bit as important for students as developing the skills required to implement them. Without these values, little use exists for the skills.

Getting Beyond the Self

Sadly, it is during exactly those years when we would like to see students discovering what is important and worthwhile to learn about in the world that other, less salutary influences are at work. Usually by middle childhood and certainly by early adolescence, children have become interested in what they can do in the outside world. But the social influences on them lead to their focusing more on what each encounter tells them about themselves than on what it tells them about the world. By middle school at the latest, children are concerned to know, "How good am I at this?" and especially, "How good am I at this compared to others?" The conclusions they draw shape both their interests and their self-image. If the conclusion is "not very good," why risk the further involvement that could reveal incompetence to others? Fueling this conclusion is the view of ability as a fixed entity that a person applies rather than develops through effort and practice.

Even on occasions when the answer to "How good am I at this?" is favorable—that is, the child does relatively well—the effect is not all we would hope. The focus remains on the self—"This is something I'm good at that will allow me to show myself in a good light." Overshadowed in both the "competent" and "incompetent" scenarios is interest in the activity itself and the opportunity it affords to learn something about the world rather than only about the self. We saw in the extreme case of students at the best-practice school how constant assessment and evaluation foster a focus on performing well relative to others, to the extent that doing so becomes an end in itself. With all of the focus on how one is doing, little attention is left to contemplate what one is doing.

Here, again, adults have a powerful role to play in communicating implicitly to students what is and is not worth attending to. They must convey through their own actions the value of the activities they engage students in and the potential for learning that these activities offer. At the same time, they need to communicate through their own actions and words the concerns that are less important and less deserving of attention. There is a place for "how am I doing?" in a great many areas of life. The challenge is that it not crowd out the more critical questions of "what am I doing?" and "why?"

Mapping the Developmental Terrain

Figure 9.1 offers a graphic summary of all of the kinds of development we would like to see—skills, understanding, and values. Students need to develop facility in the fundamental skills of inquiry (which encompass analysis and inference) and argument—the skills that will enable them to seek and acquire knowledge and to use it to make sound judgments. They also need two kinds of meta-level knowing—knowing *about* knowing. One is procedural metaknowing about their own knowledge-seeking skills, so they can deploy, monitor, and manage them optimally. The other is declarative metaknowing—understanding of the more general nature of knowledge and knowing. Critical to the latter is the progression in epistemological understanding described in Chapter 2, from regarding knowledge as facts and then opinions to understanding knowledge as judgments informed by evidence and deliberation. This is the progression that provides a foundation for the development of intellectual values.

Is it possible to ensure all of this will happen? No, but as educators, we can enhance the likelihood that it will by engaging with students as role models and partners in activities that call for these kinds of thinking. If we are successful, their orientation in inquiry will shift from one of producing outcomes or illustrating prior beliefs to one of analysis and understanding, and their orientation in argument will shift from winning to knowing.

In the process, we can support meta-level development by encouraging students to reflect on and evaluate what they do. Doing so heightens interest in the purpose of their activities. Why are we doing this? What did we gain by doing it? Is the dividend worth the investment? Questions such as these are less likely to arise when activities are imposed by authority figures without negotiation, and especially when the activities serve as occasions for evaluating students' standing relative to one another—the purpose that so often becomes an end in itself, stealing attention from any other.

With sustained engagement in activities involving competing claims and conflicting evidence, students eventually come to appreciate that all is not in fact equal, that one idea can have more merit than another, that unexamined beliefs are not worth having. This is the epistemological understanding that supports intellectual values. These new levels of understand-

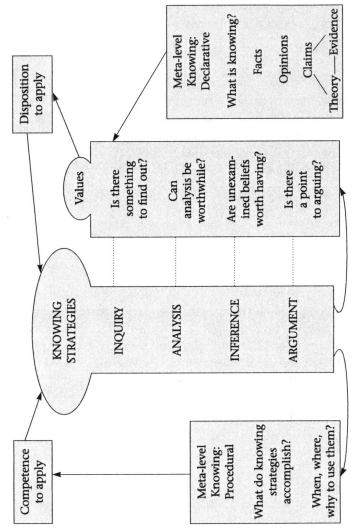

Figure 9.1. Developing skills, understanding, and values. From D. Kuhn (2001). How do people know? *Psychological Science, 12,* 1–8.

ing and valuing in turn support further engagement. Hence, engagement, valuing, and understanding bootstrap one another, each supporting the development of the other.

Can we document that students who develop this constellation of skills, understanding, and values will lead more effective or fulfilled adult lives? No, not definitively, not at present. We have too few data, and negligible data of the necessary long-term longitudinal sort, involving students whose first decade of school experience has been built on such a foundation. My argument is only that such a curriculum is feasible and our best bet for educating students for life.

I turn now to a question I have had little to say about thus far. How does an educational agenda like the one represented in Figure 9.1 connect to the standard middle-school curriculum?

Situating Inquiry and Argument in a Horizontal and Vertical Curriculum

Few educators quarrel with the idea of fostering students' thinking skills. But they embrace many other goals, both curricular and extracurricular; and by the time students reach middle school, it is a challenge to do everything. Not a minute of students' time is wasted, we saw at the best-practice school, and teachers in the different subject areas compete for a greater piece of the students' school day "pie." Students at the struggling school, in contrast, spend too much time doing not much of anything; but even so, their school day and week is divided into many short blocks of time, and they must frequently and rapidly shift locations and attention. At both schools, not all classes meet every day, and some meet as infrequently as twice a week. At neither school do students have much opportunity to get deeply involved in any activity over a sustained period, with the possible exception of sports teams at the best-practice school. Adding the agenda represented in Figure 9.1 on top of all that's going on does not appear a promising prospect. Nor does the approach I argued against earlier—attempting to infuse thinking-skill objectives unobtrusively into the regular curriculum.

The goal, moreover, is not simply to make it all fit, but to make it fit well. Continuity and integration across the curriculum are matters of primary concern to contemporary curriculum specialists. The objective is a curriculum that is seamless, with links in place at every intersection and in two directions—horizontally (across subject areas) and vertically (across grade levels). And so let us examine each direction in turn in considering how inquiry and argument might be situated in a broad curricular context having multiple objectives.

Horizontal Integration

In the horizontal direction, we encounter a traditional set of school subjects. Here we can simultaneously make two strong claims. First, inquiry and argument have a place in every one of these subject areas. Second, broad cognitive skills like inquiry and argument warrant an identity and place of their own in the curriculum structure. The first of these claims is the less controversial. All of the traditional subjects—science and Social Studies, certainly, but also reading, writing, and mathematics—entail both inquiry and argument. Indeed, much of the emphasis in both mathematics and reading has shifted from procedural skills to conceptual understanding. In mathematics, this means knowing how you know (meta-level awareness) and showing how you know (argument). In reading, it means reading to learn and understand, which in turn entails hypothesis generation, prediction, and interpretation, not simply mechanical processing of text.

Underlying the second, more controversial claim is the view that the traditional curriculum—the segmentation into subject areas based on *what* is being studied—ought not remain cast in stone and stands to benefit from being revisited regularly. Although there is much we still do not know, we know much more about the process of learning than we knew fifty years ago. Is it not at least possible that these insights support some reorganization of what is to be learned? Yet negligible change has taken place in this respect in the last century. American high-school students today still study largely the same set of subjects their grandparents did.

The traditional divisions into different subject areas have arisen from cutting the pie at a surface level—the object of study is numbers or words, the physical or the social, fact or fiction. Modern cognitive science has enabled us to go at least some distance below the surface in understanding what kinds of knowledge students may be acquiring. One consequence has been to make the surface-level borders between subject areas more permeable. The other has been to make visible conceptual unities that lie just beneath this surface. The latter become candidates for inclusion in the curriculum as subjects in their own right.

One example is causality. In Chapter 4, I described evidence suggesting that middle-school students have immature mental models of causality itself (not just of particular phenomena that involve causality). Notably, they tend not to regard causes as operating consistently in producing their effects across instances, nor to recognize multiple causes as operating additively on an outcome. Why, then, not identify causality as an area of understanding in which curricular effort is warranted? Surely the concept of causality is significant enough to justify the attention.

Working against such a step is the fact that causality as a topic does not fit neatly anywhere within the existing curriculum. I noted in Chapter 5 the decision to situate the inquiry learning program described there primarily within the area of physical science because that choice made teachers feel most assured that students were engaged with worthwhile content. Our own preference in these efforts, however, is to employ content that does not fall within traditional curriculum boundaries, such as predicting sports skill or planning a town (two current topics we are developing) or the music club scenario described in Chapter 5. In so doing, there is less danger of forgetting that the objective of the activity is not learning about the particular content as much as it is learning about inquiry.

Most desirable would be for students to engage in such inquiry on causality over the entire range of curriculum subject matter. Students would become familiar with a variety of different topics; but, most importantly, they would begin to see some of the deeper links across them. By examining causality in a biological context, a geographical context, a mechanical context, an interpersonal context, a sociological context, and any number of other contexts, students begin to understand and appreciate features of causality itself.

Vertical Integration

Vertical integration of inquiry and argument extends in two directions. Integration downward (to the early elementary and preschool years) is clearer and requires less discussion than integration upward (to the high-school years and beyond). Inquiry skills extend downward to emergence during the preschool years of the recognition of false belief—the awareness that assertions, as the product of human thought, need not accurately represent reality and therefore demand evaluation. Argument skills extend downward to the earliest efforts to prevail through reason.

With respect to the upward direction of integration of inquiry and argument skills in the curriculum, the path may be less apparent. In fact, some might conclude that the cognitive skills identified in earlier chapters are so rudimentary that they have little relevance to the cognitive demands of high school or college. Yet we cannot count on these skills to be functional in adolescents or even adults, no matter how rudimentary they may seem.

When these skills are called for in contexts only slightly richer and more elaborated, their relevance to the cognitive demands in the lives of average adults becomes apparent. Chapters 4 and 7 contain examples of the efforts of urban community college students to examine evidence of the sort that might appear in newspaper or magazine articles and to coordinate it with potential claims. In many cases, their skills were sadly lacking. Only a small percentage of students at the struggling school are destined to succeed academically to the extent of becoming students at these same community colleges. But even those who do, it appears, may not master skills they need to interpret newspapers articles on issues that affect their lives.

Despite their rudimentary nature, the cognitive skills we have examined form a continuous vertical link to intellectual skills that are clearly of a higher order. This is clearer, perhaps, in the case of argument: Counterargument to an opponent's position and rebuttal of an opponent's counterarguments are obviously essential building blocks for extended, complex, sophisticated arguments. It is easy to envision all of the gradations in between.

In the case of inquiry skills, extensions of the causal structure of the inquiry environment to interactive and probabilistic effects are noted in Chapter 5. Now envision one further extension to multiple outcome variables. For example, what if students were asked to work as town planners and to investigate the effects of various features of towns on the quality of life, as assessed by a set of different indicators (for example, survey results, civic participation, mobility data)? Students would be asked to secure data and construct an argument regarding the effect of a feature on the quality of life (as assessed by one or more indicators of the student's choice)? It is easy to imagine the potential for debate as students present their arguments (based on different outcome indicators). It is at this juncture, then, that we witness the intersection of inquiry and argument. Moreover, the inquiry and argument skills that are called for are far from elementary.

In sum, the vertical continuity of inquiry and argument skills is as robust and as seamless as their horizontal continuity. Indeed, our claim that developing these skills constitutes education for life, not just more school, rests on the exercise of inquiry and argument proving as useful to middle-aged adults as to schoolchildren. Many middle-aged (and, for that matter, younger) adults are not as inquiring or argumentive as we might like them to be. But there can be little disagreement about the potential significance of these skills to their lives. This potential provides all the reason to seek to develop these skills from an early age and to continue to support their development to the highest possible levels.

The Courage to Question

Educators—from novice classroom teacher to state superintendent—have many laudable educational goals for their students. I have argued that the skills of inquiry and argument warrant a prominent place in any of these agendas, both as entities in their own right and as a framework for all that students do. How might educators best proceed on a path of educating for thinking? In several ways, I suggest. The first, and perhaps most crucial, is summoning the courage to go back (and keep going back) to the drawing board to reexamine long-standing assumptions and traditions, rather than taking them as givens. The second is making use of the best available roadmaps of the directions in which students' thinking skills develop. These roadmaps provide the essential markers that define and illuminate the path. And the third is to avoid the temptation of side roads that appear to provide easy answers but are in fact dead ends.

Passing the Buck

We first address these side roads. What do we reply to educators who object, proclaiming, no, it can't possibly be done—education for thinking is just one more fad to be added on to all they are trying to do. We've already over-committed ourselves to too many curricular goals; students' and teachers' time and attention are diverted in too many disparate directions. We cannot add causality or argument or inquiry or anything else to an already over-stuffed curriculum.

Educators who take this perspective, I propose, must be nudged back to the drawing board, to reexamine long-held assumptions and traditions and to ask anew just why it is we do it this way. Teachers seek the most effective ways to teach what they have come to believe their students should learn, but they seldom ask themselves or others whether and why these are the most important things for students to be learning. These are matters that others have decided.

Curriculum standards have become so institutionalized that teachers can scarcely be blamed for the buck-passing that has become commonplace in modern education: Teachers teach what principals and superintendents dictate they should; and these administrators in turn are bound by curriculum standards dictated by district and state education departments, who will judge their schools by how well test scores indicate these standards are being met. In a different form of buck-passing, but similar in consequences, elementary school teachers see their task as preparing students for the demands of middle school, while middle-school teachers seek to prepare students for high-school and high-school teachers to prepare students for college. And ultimately college educators are left to debate the goals of an increasingly costly undergraduate education.

This book rests on the argument that somewhere—in public and private colleges or in state superintendents' offices, and most likely in all of these places—we need to set aside these dictates long enough to take fresh looks at our most basic goals. What do we want students to know or be able to do by the time they have completed the years of universal schooling, and why? How do we justify our answers to these questions? Education toward what end? In the face of these questions, curriculum priorities can shift radically.

How likely to occur are these fresh looks and the changes they may suggest? On the positive side, the sense of a need for change is widespread. No less a contemporary figure than Bill Gates has claimed that American high schools are obsolete. Rather than any disagreement or debate, the major consequence of Gates's 2005 proclamation to an education coalition of governors of eighteen states (with more promised to join) was resolve to address this problem. On the less encouraging side are the governors' ideas of what to do. Gates (2005) told them students need "a challenging curriculum that prepares them for college or work; that their course relate to their lives and goals; and that they are surrounded by adults who push them to achieve." The governors responded by pledging to adopt "higher standards, more rigorous courses and tougher examinations." Missing here, of course, and unlikely to arise from the governors' coalition, is thought about what kind of curriculum will prepare students for the future lives and goals Gates talks about. Aiming at higher standards, more rigorous courses and tougher examinations—doing what we now do but doing it better—ignores the question. An irony that cannot be escaped here is that Gates' own professional success came from creating something new, ushering in a revolution that has changed lives around the world.

What Is Best?

Does comparison of the best-practice and struggling-school classrooms offer any insight into these matters? Most parents, given the choice, would opt to have their children attend the best-practice school, despite its pressured atmosphere. But does it in fact reflect the "best practice" we are capable of?

If we talk, as I did, to those who receive most of the credit for the best-practice school's performance—the middle-school and high-school principals and the district superintendent—or listen to their public presentations, their stance is clear. "Ours is a standard of excellence," the leaders of the best-practice school say, "that we can rightfully be proud of and must continually work to maintain." How do they know how excellent their school is? Here the familiar indicators are recited, not just by these leaders, but by everyone in the community—highest SAT scores of any public school in the county, greatest number of AP courses taken with the best scores, most prestigious college placement record, and so forth.

Does the school deserve to congratulate itself over these statistics? Well, yes, it would seem, but with the recognition that when you are winning, you are disinclined to take too close a look at why. And you are certainly disinclined to change much of anything—just stay on your toes and be sure not to let standards slip. I was struck by the parallel between this stance on the part of the school's leaders and the stance on the part of students that we noted to be particularly strong at the best-practice school: "How I am doing" relative to others is the single indicator that defines accomplishment. This comparative focus, we found, dominated to the extent of obscuring attention to some other worthy questions—notably, *what* it is I am doing, and why.

At the individual level, the comparative stance works against what I have referred to as the development of intellectual values. If I am performing better than most at the tasks I am given, I am less likely to worry about whether these are the tasks most worth doing. Performing them well confers such a positive self-image as to make any further reasons for engaging in them unnecessary.

At the institutional level, this same stance works against the kind of reflective examination that serves as a path to progress. If we do not continue to reflect openly on what we are doing, we are unlikely to see how it might be changed. Ironically, it is the schools with the most resources, and hence flexibility to innovate, that are least willing to risk change. They are responsible to communities who would be up in arms if performance dipped even slightly. And so things that seem to be working stay in place. Schools at the other end of the performance spectrum, in comparison, like the struggling school, more likely see themselves as having little to lose in undertaking change, but they typically lack the resources or collective will to do so in any concerted way.

The parallel between the comparative focus at the individual and at the institutional level is likely not accidental. In any case, the message we ought to emphasize to students is one that the adults around them might take heed of as well. Comparison with others does not make one best. We cannot determine what "best" is in that fashion.

Put differently, "best practice" must be understood to mean "best prevailing practice," not "best possible practice." We might even go so far as to suggest that there is as much room for improvement at the best-practice school as there is at the struggling school, despite their very different positions. At the best-practice school, eleven- and twelve-year-olds become accomplished at registering, organizing, and managing impressive quantities of information. Yet their understanding of "why it's important to know this" is as much in need of development as is that of the struggling-school students who appear to be learning so much less. Neither group has been able to make much genuine meaning of their school experience.

Sharing and Refining Roadmaps

At both individual and institutional levels, roadmaps are needed of where one is going and why, as well as the flexibility and courage to reexamine and refine the map, and even revise it when new roads are identified. Students, I have argued, must be part of the planning enterprise. They, as much as the adults who guide them, must construct a vision of where they are going and why.

These educational roadmaps reflect a base of psychological knowledge regarding the patterns, sequences, and endpoints that characterize the intellectual development we would like to see. Intellectual skills develop slowly and with practice. They are not simply supplied to students as items from a ready-to-use toolkit. No teacher can work that kind of magic. Teachers need to have a clear sense of where intellectual development is headed, the milestones along the way, and the processes that allow it to happen.

Without such roadmaps, teachers may be resourceful to varying degrees in devising classroom activities that appear to engage children's minds. But they can have at best a rough sense of what their efforts are accomplishing. Few would question the claim that teachers need to know how children's thinking develops. Indeed, it's widely assumed that they acquire such knowledge as part of their teacher training. In truth, teachers' own education about either the broad patterns or the details of their students' cognitive development is typically sketchy at best. In what has become a familiar refrain, there just is not room for it in the curriculum.

The roadmaps of students' developing inquiry and argument skills that I offer in earlier chapters are far from definitive. They need to be refined, elaborated, and corrected in the course of what is now called design-based research (Cobb et al., 2003)—that is, research in which the dual goals of instructional design and theory development are intertwined. In this work, psychologists are not merely the technicians who come in to advise educators how best to achieve their instructional goals. Rather, they are deeply involved in the articulation of those goals.

Education for All

In Chapter 1, I noted the formidable challenge that universal public education poses. What unifying educational experience can be justified as serving the needs of the increasingly diverse segments of our society? Contrasts between the best-practice and struggling schools make the extent of that segmentation painfully clear. Education in American urban centers has truly become a juxtaposition of two unconnected worlds, the world of the privileged and the world of those who do without. This situation can be changed. But doing so will require enormous effort, investment, commitment, and resolve, at so many levels of society that it is hard to envision the coordination that will make it happen. The disadvantaged "at risk" segment of American children for the most part get enough nourishment that they do not suffer the physical starvation suffered by so many of their counterparts in third world countries. But these American children are at least malnourished, if not starved, intellectually. When I returned to the struggling school a year later, conditions were worse than I'd found them the year before, with the principal transferred out of the school a month into the school year, a third of the teachers new to the school, and class sizes of 40 and more students—and this in the era of "No Child Left Behind."

Changing this situation requires action at a political level. There are promising signs, like the governors' coalition noted earlier, that the necessary political will exists. Yet it remains the province of educators to identify the educational goals, as well as the methods, that can best serve the needs of children and society. Herein lies the promise of universal education—to function as leveler, as well as sorter, by providing the members of a society with a unifying experience that is enhancing and valuable to all.

Inquiry and argument are competencies of value to students from all segments of society. Even more than competencies, they are ways of knowing the world and of acting on and within it. Moreover, they are ways of knowing and acting that we would equally like to see develop in young people from the most and the least privileged segments of society. For all of the striking differences in their past, present, and future lives, it is here that students from the best-practice and struggling schools are able to share a common set of goals. The evidence presented in this book, moreover, shows that they are goals as much within the reach of one group as the other. We did not find students at the best-practice school models of perfection or so far ahead as to be without rival with respect to the skills identified in this book, as they are in more visible indicators like SAT scores and college admissions. Education for thinking, then, is indeed a unifying education for all.

Education As a Sense-Making Partnership

The proposals I have made in this book are, on the one hand, radical, calling for change at the highest level. On the other hand, they articulate a perspective and framework that can be of value even to those classroom teachers who do not have the autonomy to set their own curricular objectives or design their own lesson plans.

At the highest policy level, much is not working well—is not making sense—I have suggested, with respect to the standard middle- and high-school curriculum, and this is so across the educational spectrum, from its most elite to least advantaged segments. This curriculum warrants a hard, unforgiving look, with preconceptions set aside. "It's always been done this way" should not be accorded any argumentive force. Replacing tradition, the hard questions about long-term objectives must come to the fore.

The education for thinking that I have proposed is education for life; and, fully implemented, it differs significantly from the conventional curriculum. The conclusion that students would become better educated if they were to "cover" less material in a deeper and different kind of way, at the expense perhaps of some subjects that have been in the school curriculum for generations, is a radical policy conclusion that will not be reached easily and will require great courage on the part of those who seek to realize it.

At the same time, those who labor within the existing education system and, at least at the moment, are not in a position to change it stand to gain from an appreciation of two themes highlighted in this book. One is the critical importance of intellectual activities that have broad, intrinsic value that becomes evident in the course of engaging them. They are the skills students will become sold on and take with them as education for life. As teachers, we must further our understanding of the nature of these fundamental thinking skills and how they develop, so we can have our eye on them in everyday life in the classroom.

The second theme is that educators must become partners with students who seek to become educated. In the end, students must make sense of, and must take charge of, their own education. We have only a brief window of opportunity to engage their trust that we are indeed partners in this enterprise—that we will not waste their time and will ask them to do only those things that are worth doing. And so we must consider and choose very carefully what we ask students to do, if we are to gain and keep that trust. We also must seek to focus their attention away from how they are doing compared to others and instead on what they are doing and what it means.

What students think they are doing is much more important than what we think we want to teach them. With sustained engagement, they will come to believe that inquiry and argument offer the most promising path to resolving conflicts, solving problems, and achieving goals. They will become convinced that there are things to find out, that analysis is worthwhile, that unexamined beliefs are not worth having. These are intellectual values, complementary to but distinct from intellectual skills. Engagement, valuing, and understanding bootstrap one another. Yet values, in the end, may be the most critical of the three because students themselves will ultimately decide what is worth knowing. They must find the reasons to become educated. If they do not, schools will experience mediocre success at best.

REFERENCES

Ahn, W., and Bailenson, J. (1996). Causal attribution a a search for underlying mechanisms: An explanation of the conjunction fallacy and the discounting principle. *Cognitive Psychology, 31,* 82–123.

Ahn, W., Kalish, C., Medin, D., and Gelman, S. (1995). The role of covariation versus mechanism information in causal attribution. *Cognition, 54,* 299–352.

Anderson, N. (1991). *Contributions to information integration theory.* Vol. III: *Development.* Mahwah, NJ: Erlbaum.

Anderson, J., Greeno, J., Reder, L., and Simon, H. (2000). Perspectives on learning, thinking, and activity. *Educational Researcher, 29,* 11–13.

Bereiter, C. (2002). *Education and mind in the knowledge age.* Mahwah, NJ: Erlbaum.

Billig, M. (1987). *Arguing and thinking: A rhetorical approach to social psychology.* Cambridge: Cambridge University Press.

Botstein, L. (1997). *Jefferson's children: Education and the promise of American culture.* New York: Doubleday.

Bransford, J., Brown, A., and Cocking, R. (eds.). (1999). *How people learn: Brain, mind, experience, and school.* Report of the National Research Council. Washington, DC: National Academy Press.

Brem, S., and Rips, L. (2000). Explanation and evidence in informal argument. *Cognitive Science, 24,* 573–604.

Brewer, W., and Samarapungavan, A. (1991). Children's theories vs. scientific theories: Differences in reasoning or differences in knowledge. In R. Hoffman and D. Palermo (eds.), *Cognition and the symbolic processes.* Hillsdale, NJ: Erlbaum.

Brown, A. (1997). Transforming schools into communities of thinking and learning about serious matters. *American Psychologist, 52,* 399–413.

Chandler, M., and Lalonde, C. (2003). Representational diversity redux. Paper presented at the biennial meeting of the Society for Research in Child Development, Tampa, FL.

Cobb, P., Confrey, J., diSessa, A., Lehrer, R., and Schauble, L. (2003). Design experiments in educational research. *Educational Researcher, 32,* 9–13.

Dewey, J. (1916). *Democracy and education: An introduction to the philosophy of education.* In J. Boydston (ed.), *The middle works of John Dewey* (Vol. 9). Carbondale, IL: Southern Illinois University Press.

de Jong, T., and van Joolingen, W. R. (1998). Scientific discovery learning with computer simulations of conceptual domains. *Review of Educational Research, 68,* 179–201.

Dixon, J., and Tuccillo, F. (2001). Generating initial models for reasoning. *Journal of Experimental Child Psychology, 78,* 178–212.

Dweck, C., and Leggett, E. (1988). A social-cognitive approach to motivation and personality. *Psychological Review, 95,* 256–273.

Edelson, D., Gordon, D., and Pea, R. (1999). Addressing the challenge of inquiry-based learning. *Journal of the Learning Sciences, 8,* 392–450.

Eisenhart, M., Finkel, E., and Marion, S. (1996). Creating the conditions for scientific literacy: A re-examination. *American Educational Research Journal, 33,* 261–295.

Felton, M. (2004). The development of discourse strategies in adolescent argumentation. *Cognitive Development, 19,* 35–52.

Felton, M., and Kuhn, D. (2001). The development of argumentive discourse skills. *Discourse Processes, 32,* 135–153.

Fischer, K., and Bidell, T. (1991). Constraining nativist inferences about cognitive capacities. In S. Carey and R. Gelman (eds.), *The epigenesis of mind: Essays on biology and cognition.* Mahwah, NJ: Erlbaum.

Gardner, H. (1999). *The disciplined mind.* New York: Simon and Schuster.

Gates, W. (2005). What's wrong with American high schools. *LA Times,* Feb. 27, 2005.

Gelman, S. (2006). Conceptual development. In D. Kuhn and R. Siegler (eds.), *Handbook of child psychology.* Vol. 2: *Cognition, perception, and language* (6th ed.) (W. Damon and R. Lerner, series eds.). Hoboken, NJ: Wiley.

Gopnik, A., and Graf, P. (1988). Knowing how you know: Young children's ability to identify and remember the sources of their beliefs. *Child Development, 59,* 1366–1371.

Graff, G. (1992). *Beyond the culture wars: How teaching the conflicts can revitalize American education.* New York: Norton.

Graff, G. (2003). *Clueless in academe: How schooling obscures the life of the mind.* New Haven: Yale University Press.

Hirsch, E. D. (1987). *Cultural literacy: What every American needs to know.* Boston: Houghton Mifflin.

Hirsch, E. D., Kett, J., and Trefil, J. (2002). *The new dictionary of cultural literacy.* Boston: Houghton Mifflin.

Hmelo, C. E., Holton, D. L., Kolodner, J. L. (2000). Designing to learn about complex systems. *Journal of the Learning Sciences, 9*(3), 247–298.

Hofer, B., and Pintrich, P. (1997). The development of epistemological theories: Beliefs about knowledge and knowing and their relation to learning. *Review of Educational Research, 67,* 88–140.

Hofer, B., and Pintrich, P. (eds.). (2002). *Epistemology: The psychology of beliefs about knowledge and knowing.* Mahwah, NJ: Erlbaum.

Jackson, A., and Davis, G. (2000). *Turning points 2000: Educating adolescents in the 21st century.* New York: Teachers College Press.

Keating, D. (2004). Cognitive and brain development. In R. Lerner and L. Steinberg (eds.), *Handbook of adolescent psychology.* Chichester: Wiley.

Keil, F. (2006). Cognitive science and cognitive development. In D. Kuhn and R. Siegler (eds.), *Handbook of child psychology.* Vol. 2: *Cognition, perception, and language* (6th ed.) (W. Damon and R. Lerner, series eds.). Hoboken, NJ: Wiley.

Keselman, A. (2003). Promoting scientific reasoning in a computer-assisted environment. *Journal for Research in Science Teaching.*

Kinlaw, C., and Kurtz-Costes, B. (2003). The development of children's beliefs about intelligence. *Developmental Review, 23,* 125–161.

Krajcik, J., Blumenfeld, P., Marx, R., Bass, K., Fredricks, J., and Soloway, E. (1998). Inquiry in project-based science classrooms: Initial attempts by middle school students. *Journal of the Learning Sciences, 7,* 313–350.

Kuhn, D. (1989). Children and adults as intuitive scientists. *Psychological Review, 96,* 674–689.

Kuhn, D. (1991). *The skills of argument.* Cambridge: Cambridge University Press.

Kuhn, D. (1995). Microgenetic study of change: What has it told us? *Psychological Science, 6,* 133–139.

Kuhn, D. (2001). How do people know? *Psychological Science, 12,* 1–8.

Kuhn, D. (2001). Why development does (and doesn't) occur: Evidence from the domain of inductive reasoning. In R. Siegler and J. McClelland (eds.), *Mechanisms of cognitive development: Neural and behavioral perspectives.* Mahwah, NJ: Erlbaum.

Kuhn, D. (2002). What is scientific thinking and how does it develop? In U. Goswami (ed.), *Handbook of childhood cognitive development.* Oxford: Blackwell.

Kuhn, D. and Franklin, S. (2006). The second decade: What develops (and how)? In D. Kuhn and R. Siegler (eds.), *Handbook of Child Psychology.* Vol. 2: *Cognition, perception, and language* (6th ed.) (W. Damon and R. Lerner, series eds.). Hoboken, NJ: Wiley.

Kuhn, D., Amsel, E., and O'Loughlin, M. (1988). *The development of scientific thinking skills.* San Diego: Academic Press.

Kuhn, D., Black, J., Keselman, A., and Kaplan, D. (2000). The development of cognitive skills to support inquiry learning. *Cognition and Instruction, 18,* 495–523.

Kuhn, D., Cheney, R., and Weinstock, M. (2000). The development of epistemological understanding. *Cognitive Development, 15,* 309–328.

Kuhn, D., and Dean, D. (2004). Connecting scientific reasoning and causal inference. *Journal of Cognition and Development, 5,* 261–288.

Kuhn, D., and Felton, M. (2000). Paper presented at the Winter Conference on Discourse, Text, and Cognition, Jackson Hole WY.

Kuhn, D., Garcia-Mila, M., Zohar, A., and Andersen, C. (1995). *Strategies of knowledge acquisition* (with commentaries by Sheldon White, David Klahr, and Sharon Carver). *Society for Research in Child Development Monographs, 60*(4), Serial no. 245.

Kuhn, D., Katz, J., and Dean, D. (2004). Developing reason. *Thinking and Reasoning, 10,* 197–219.

Kuhn, D., and Pearsall, S. (1998). Relations between metastrategic knowledge and strategic performance. *Cognitive Development, 13,* 227–247.

Kuhn, D., and Pearsall, S. (2000). Developmental origins of scientific thinking. *Journal of Cognition and Development, 1,* 113–129.

Kuhn, D., Schauble, L., and Garcia-Mila, M. (1992). Cross-domain development of scientific reasoning. *Cognition and Instruction, 9,* 285–232.

Kuhn, D., Shaw, V., and Felton, M. (1997). Effects of dyadic interaction on argumentive reasoning. *Cognition and Instruction, 15,* 287–315.

Kuhn, D., and Udell, W. (2003). The development of argument skills. *Child Development, 74,* 1245–1260.

Levstik, L., and Barton, K. (2001). *Doing history: Investigating with children in elementary and middle schools.* Mahwah, NJ: Erlbaum.

Marx, R., Blumenfeld, P., Krajcik, J., Blunk, M., Crawford, B., Kelley, B., and Meyer, K. (1994). Enacting project-based science: Challenges for practice and policy. *Elementary School Journal, 97,* 341–358.

McGinn, M., and Roth, W. (1999). Preparing students for competent scientific practice: Implications of recent research in science and technology studies. *Educational Researcher, 28,* 14–24.

Meier, D. (1995). *The power of their ideas: Lessons for America from a small school in Harlem.* Boston: Beacon Press.

Moshman, D. (1993). Adolescent reasoning and adolescent rights. *Human Development, 36,* 27–40.

Moshman, D., and Geil, M. (1998). Collaborative reasoning: Evidence for collective rationality. *Thinking and Reasoning, 4,* 231–248.

Murnane, R., and Levy, F. (1996). *Teaching the new basic skills.* New York: Free Press.

National Research Council (1996). The National Science Education Standards. Washington, DC: National Academy Press.

National Research Council (2000). Inquiry and the National Science Education Standards: A guide for teaching and learning. Washington, DC: National Academy Press.

Nicholls, J. (1989). *The competitive ethos and democratic education.* Cambridge, MA: Harvard University Press.

Olson, D. (2003). *Psychological theory and educational reform: How school remakes mind and society.* New York: Cambridge University Press.

Olson, D., and Astington, J. (1993). Thinking about thinking: Learning how to take statements and hold beliefs. *Educational Psychologist, 28,* 7–23.

Perkins, D., Jay, E., and Tishman, S. (1993). Beyond abilities: A dispositional theory of thinking. *Merrill-Palmer Quarterly, 39,* 1–21.

Perner, J. (1991). *Understanding the representational mind.* Cambridge, MA: MIT Press.

Piaget, J. (1926). *Language and thought of the child.* New York: Harcourt Brace.

Resnick, L., Levine, H., and Teasley, S. (1991). *Perspectives on socially shared cognition.* Washington, DC: American Psychological Association.

Robinson, E. (2000). Belief and disbelief: Children's assessments of the reliability of sources of knowledge about the world. In K. Roberts and M. Blades (eds.), *Children's source monitoring.* Mahwah, NJ: Erlbaum.

Rogoff, B. (1998). Cognition as a collaborative process. In D. Kuhn and R. Siegler (eds.), *Handbook of child psychology.* Vol. 2: *Cognition, perception, and language* (5th ed.) (W. Damon, series ed.). New York: Wiley.

Schauble, L. (1990). Belief revision in children: The role of prior knowledge and strategies for generating evidence. *Journal of Experimental Child Psychology, 49,* 31–57.

Schauble, L. (1996). The development of scientific reasoning in knowledge-rich contexts. *Developmental Psychology, 32,* 102–119.

Schoenfeld, A. (1999). Looking toward the 21st century: Challenges of educational theory and practice. *Educational Researcher, 28,* 4–14.

Schwarz, B., Newman, Y., and Biezuner, S. (2000). Two wrongs may make a right. . .if they argue together. *Cognition and Instruction, 18,* 461–494.

Siegler, R. (2006). Microgenetic studies of learning. In D. Kuhn and R. Siegler (eds.), *Handbook of child psychology.* Vol. 2: *Cognition, perception, and language* (6th ed.) (W. Damon and R. Lerner, series eds.). Hoboken, NJ: Wiley.

Simon, K. (2001). *Moral questions in the classroom: How to get kids to think deeply about real life and their schoolwork.* New Haven: Yale University Press.

Sternberg, R. (1998). Abilities are forms of developing expertise. *Educational Researcher, 27,* 11–20.

Taylor, M., Esbensen, B., and Bennett, R. (1994). Children's understanding of knowledge acquisition: The tendency for children to report they have always known what they just learned. *Child Development, 65,* 1581–1604.

Walton, D. N. (1989). Dialogue theory for critical thinking. *Argumentation, 3,* 169–184.

Yeh, S. (2002). Tests worth teaching to: Constructing state-mandated tests that emphasize critical thinking. *Educational Researcher, 30,* 12–17.